Fort Edmonton Historical Foundation

An illustrated guide to

FORT EDMONTON PARK

Havelock House

Victoria, British Columbia, Canada

Book design by Havelock House
Maps supplied by the Fort Edmonton Historical Foundation

Published by:
Havelock House, 244 Moss Street
Victoria, British Columbia, Canada
V8V 4M4

Printed by Pinto Graphics, Edmonton, Alberta, Canada

00 99 98 97 96   6 5 4 3 2 1

Canadian Cataloguing in Publication Data

Main entry under title:

An illustrated guide to Fort Edmonton Park

  Includes bibliographical references and index.
  ISBN 0-920805-03-5

  1. Fort Edmonton Park (Alta.)--Guidebooks. 2. Fort Edmonton Park (Alta.)--Pictorial works. 3. Historic buildings--Alberta--Fort Edmonton Park--Guidebooks. I. Fort Edmonton Historical Foundation. FC3665.F6714 1996   971.23'34'01
C94-910596-1   F1079.F6714 1996

Fort Edmonton Park Access Routes

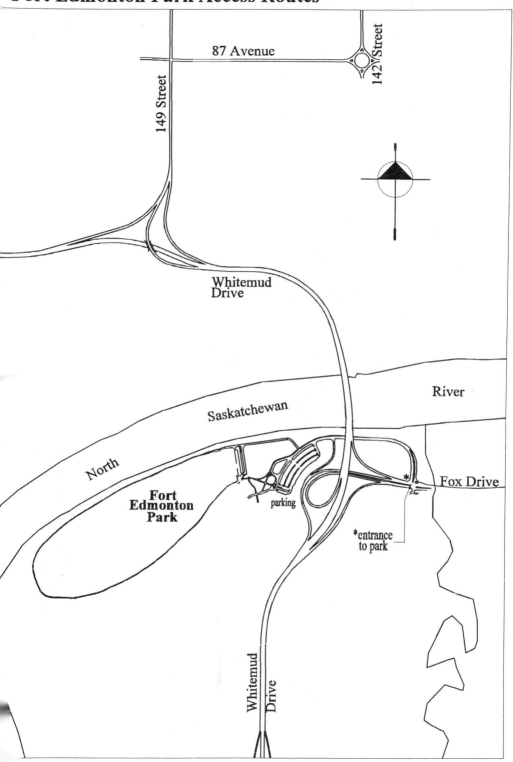

Getting around in Fort Edmonton Park

Fort Edmonton Park
Edmonton, Alberta

TABLE OF CONTENTS

GETTING THE MOST FROM A VISIT TO FORT EDMONTON PARK

Several time periods in Edmonton's development are represented in Fort Edmonton Park. Visitors who wish to progress *through time* may begin their visit with the earliest periods depicted by the Indian camp and Fort Edmonton. Simply board the steam train from the station at the Park entrance for a seven minute trip to the entrance of Fort Edmonton.

The **Indian camp** located outside Fort Edmonton represents the native tribes who lived in the area before the white man arrived. Fur trading was an important industry for many years in the Edmonton area. A replica of the Hudson's Bay Company's **Fort Edmonton** shows what life was like in a fur trading post. The next era, **1885 Street**, represents life in a small community before the coming of the railway. **1905 Street** shows Edmonton after the arrival of the railway. **1920 Street** portrays city life and industry before the Second World War.

Savour the sights and sounds and explore the dwellings and businesses of each era. Then board a vintage streetcar for a ride down 1905 and 1920 Streets and an opportunity to experience the sights of Edmonton as they may have appeared to passengers of years ago.

Visitors leaving the Park may board the streetcars on 1905 and 1920 Streets and disembark near the Park entrance at the train station.

HANDY THINGS TO KNOW!

FOOD SERVICES
Picnic tables and benches are located throughout the Park. Light snacks or hearty pioneer fare may be purchased at:

Fort Edmonton
Trading Post - soda pop and snacks
1885 Street
Jasper House - full meals, licensed
Kelly's Saloon - soda pop, snacks
Lauder's Bakery - breads, pastries
1905 Street
Masonic Hall - short order menu
1920 Street
Bill's Confectionery - soda fountain,
ice cream

LOST AND FOUND
Administration Office in the Train Station. Telephone **496-8777** during working hours.

LOST CHILDREN/PARENTS
Any Park employee will help.

EMERGENCIES OR FIRST AID
Any Park employee will help.

TELEPHONES
Train Station at the Park entrance, Masonic Hall, or the Trading Post.

STROLLERS
rental and return - Trading Post or Train Station.

WASHROOMS
- All ground level washrooms (*) are disabled accessible and have baby changing stations.
Fort - Columbia House*
1885 Street - McDougall's General Store,* Kelly's Saloon, Egge's Bunkhouse*
1905 Street - Masonic Hall, Gyro Playground, Firehall
1920 Street - Sun Drugs,* Station

THINGS TO DO AT THE PARK ·

Note: Not all activities are available every day. Please ask the staff or consult the daily schedule of events available at the entrance to the park.

On many weekends there are special activities taking place throughout the Park. Please check the daily schedule.

There is a charge for activities marked with an *.

FORT EDMONTON

Lake and Creek System
Enjoy a picnic beside the lake and watch the ducks.

Hudson's Bay Company Fort
Listen to the storyteller tell stories of the fur trade.
Tell the time using the sundial in front of Rowand House.
Watch a Red River cart being loaded for a trip (See daily schedule).
Find out how to bale furs using the fur press.
See what a fur trading store looked like many years ago.
Smell bread being baked in the outdoor oven (See daily schedule).

Indian Camp
Taste the bannock.
Watch furs being scraped. (occasionally)
Watch beading.

Trading Post
*Ride a pony, the stage coach, or a wagon (tickets at the Trading Post).
*Shop for souvenirs.
*Enjoy a soft drink from the soft drink machine.
Pat a pony at the pony ride (watch their teeth).

1885 STREET

Ottewell farm
   Watch the pigs play . . . or sleep.
   Learn how to walk on stilts.
   Wave to the scarecrow.
   Ride a hobby horse.
   Skip rope.
   Play with toys from the 1800s.
   See the chickens and turkeys up close.

See a one-room school of the 1800s (Bellerose School).
Read the news from 1885, or
   *Get your name printed on a wanted poster at the *Bulletin*
      newspaper office.
Visit the museum in the McDougall Methodist Church and listen
   to music on the old-time organ.
* Shop at McDougall's General Store for shaving needs, old-time
      enamelled kitchenware and other household items.
Be part of the audience as an historical scene is re-enacted.
      (Please check daily schedule.)
* Enjoy a cookie or other baked goods at Lauder's bakeshop.
* Shop for old-time china and rock candy at Daly's Drugstore.
Play billiards in the billiard room behind Kelly's saloon.
   *Get a (soft) drink at Kelly's Saloon.
   Play the piano at Kelly's - (Get permission first from the staff.)
Watch the blacksmith at work in the blacksmith shop.
* Have lunch at the Jasper House hotel.
See how small a cell was in the jail behind the North-West
      Mounted Police Station.
Visit a settler's campsite and hear tales of the trail.

Egge's Stopping House
   Ride a rocking horse on the porch.
   Sample the cakes and cooking.
   Listen to story telling.

Things to do

1905 STREET

Ride on the streetcar.
Pat the horses at the Henderson round barn.
Ring the bell at the Firehall.
Bring your lunch and have a picnic at the picnic tables.
Play on the swings and teeter-totters at Gyro Park.
* Enjoy a snack in the Masonic Hall.
Visit the Masonic Lodge museum upstairs in the Masonic Hall.
Watch the Temperance march. (please check schedule of events)
* Have your palm read or test your strength at the Penny Arcade.
* Try your shooting skill at the Shooting Gallery.
Sit on the grass and listen to live music or watch a play at the East
  End Bandshell. (please check schedule of events)
See the flowers at Ramsay's greenhouse.
* Purchase postcards, stamps, and stamp boxes at the Post Office.
* Shop for souvenirs and gifts at Reed's Bazaar.
Look at photographs of early Edmonton taken by Ernest Brown at
  the Ernest Brown Studio.
* Have your photograph taken in old style clothes at Brown's studio.
  (Please check daily schedule.)
See the jail at the Firehall.
See where Edmonton's town meetings were held (upstairs in the
  Firehall).
Take a tour through 1905 and 1920 Streets on the *Seeing
  Edmonton* sightseeing bus or a vintage automobile. (Please
  check schedule of events.)

1920 STREET

Relax on a bench at the Memorial Garden. Watch the fountain
  and enjoy the flowers.

Ukrainian Bookstore (Some activities depend on staff available.)
  Listen to Ukrainian music.
  Learn how to decorate Ukrainian Easter eggs.
  Learn how to do cross-stitch.
  Play with the wooden bear toys or the Natroshka dolls.

* indicates an activity for which there is a charge.

1920 STREET (continued)

* Enjoy an ice cream cone, soda, or sundae at Bill's Confectionery.
* Play miniature golf at the Tom Thumb miniature Golf Course.
  Talk to the past on an antique telephone or watch a telephone
      operator operate the switchboard at the AGT Telephone
      Exchange.
  Wave at the train crew as the train goes by.
  See the steam tractor at the Mellon Farm.
  Pat the horses at the Mellon Farm.
  Watch a threshing machine at work. (Annual harvest fair only -
      check calendar of events for the date.)
  Ride the train.
  Visit the gift shop in the Train Station.
  Sit on the station platform and watch the train come in.
  Listen to music or watch a live performance on the station platform.
  Ring the locomotive bell on the station platform.
  Watch the trains on the model railway at the Freight Shed.
      (weekends only)

AFTER YOUR VISIT

Now that you have more time, read about the history of the
buildings which you saw at the Park.

Use the maps in the guidebook on pages 55 and 100 to visit
the original locations in Edmonton of some of the buildings
which you have seen in the Park. A few of the buildings are
still at their original sites. See the guidebook for more
information.

Tell a friend about your visit to Fort Edmonton Park.
We'd like to be able to welcome them, too.

7

FORT EDMONTON - FUR TRADING ERA (1795 - 1870)

The demand for furs began in Europe in the 1500s, first for the manufacture of fur garments and later for felt hats. The beaver pelt was the most valued for hat-making, as the tiny barbs on the underfur of this animal produced the most tightly-matted felt. The beaver-felt hat was in turn prized for its quality, and its possession served as a mark of rank within the social order. Among North American fur traders the value of trade goods soon came to be calculated in terms of beaver pelts.

The fur trade in Canada had its beginning in the 16th century when fishermen coming to the east coast were offered furs by the native peoples in exchange for much-prized European goods. Later, in western Canada, the fur industry flourished until settlers whose main interest was farming poured into the region in the 19th century.

In Canada, two major fur-trading companies eventually be-

Fort Edmonton in 1871 near the present Alberta legislature

came the main competitors in this valuable trade: the Hudson's Bay Company, founded in England, May 2, 1670 under a royal charter, and the North West Company, founded at Montreal in 1779. Under its charter, the Hudson's Bay Company held exclusive trading rights in all lands draining into Hudson Bay, the territory known as Rupert's Land. The Company established fur trading posts along the shores of Hudson Bay but initially did not move inland.

Small independent traders from Montreal began to move into the west

Fort Edmonton, Legislature Buildings, and City

along what is now the Canada-United States border, and from there north into the Hudson's Bay Company's land, intercepting the Hudson Bay-bound furs before they left the area.

The Hudson's Bay Company soon realized that the number of furs being brought to its posts along the shores of Hudson Bay was declining. Since the independent traders did not recognize the Hudson's Bay Company's charter, and the company had no means of enforcing it, its directors made a decision to move inland from the shores of Hudson Bay. The first Hudson's Bay Company inland trading post was Cumberland House, built in 1774 on the Saskatchewan River close to the present Manitoba-Saskatchewan boundary. Over the next twenty-five years the Hudson's Bay Company and the newly-formed North West Company moved further and further inland, indulging in what became ruinous competition for both, but especially for the Hudson's Bay Company.

Eventually, the directors of the two companies realized that over time such competition would be unprofitable. As a result, on March 26, 1821, an act of Parliament established a coalition of the two under the name of the Hudson's Bay Company.

The first Hudson's Bay Company post in the Edmonton area, Edmonton House, was built in 1795 near what is now Fort Saskatchewan. Earlier the same year the North West Company built the nearby post of Fort Augustus. At that time, the territories of the former company included the Arctic, which could be reached by way of the Athabasca River, Lake Athabasca, and the mighty Mackenzie River. The Athabasca River came as close as 129 kilometres (eighty miles) to the Edmonton area. The company's trading areas also included the Columbia District, a region which stretched from California to Alaska on the western side of the Rocky Mountains. The furs which reached Edmonton House from the Arctic and the Columbia District were combined with furs obtained from tribes in the vicinity of the fort and transported by York boat to Hudson Bay for shipment to England. Edmonton House therefore became an important link in a great fur gathering network which at its peak covered half a continent.

The original site of Edmonton House was unsatisfactory, and in 1802 both Edmonton House (later called Fort Edmonton) and Fort Augustus were rebuilt on a site near the present main power plant on the Rossdale flats in Edmonton. From 1810 to 1813 another location eighty kilometres (fifty miles) downstream was tried. The two forts then returned to the city area, probably near Victoria Park.

By 1821 the two trading companies had amalgamated, and by 1830 recurring high floods and the generally poor condition of both fur posts forced a relocation of Fort Edmonton to its last site on what are now the grounds of the Alberta legislature. The reproduction of Fort Edmonton at Fort Edmonton Park most closely resembles the final structure as it appeared about 1846.

Unfortunately for the fur trading industry, fashions change. Felt hats made from beaver pelts which had been so popular among the upper classes of society gave place to silk hats which came into

11

fashion about 1824. By the 1840s the increasing use of silk began to have an impact on the demand for furs. After 1870 when the bulk of the land held by the Hudson's Bay Company was sold to the new Dominion of Canada, the company found a new role as a supplier of goods to the settlers who flocked to the area

As a result of this changed role, Fort Edmonton was able to survive for a time. However, the profits from this type of commerce were nowhere near the amounts obtained from the fur trade. Consequently in 1915 the old fort was finally dismantled.

FORT EDMONTON

Palisades and Bastions. The six metre (twenty foot) high palisade or wall which enclosed all of the fort buildings was constructed as protection for the inhabitants of the fort. A walkway about 1.2 metres (four feet) below the top of the palisade allowed the company's men to observe the area surrounding the fort. On the river side of the palisade, the massive inner and outer

The palisades and bastions

gates marked the main entrance. There were also gates by the gentlemen's horse yard and the bachelors' quarters.

A square, two-story structure called a bastion was constructed at each of the palisade's four corners. The height of each bastion was 10.7 metres (thirty-five feet). The first story was 2.7 metres (nine feet) above the ground, the second, about 6.4 metres (twenty-one feet), just slightly below the walkways. Wide ladders inside the bastions were used for access to the two floors as well as to the walkway. Gunpowder for the small cannon used to greet trading parties of native people was sometimes stored in the bastions.

Indian House. For the purpose of the fur trade, the Indian House was undoubtedly the most significant structure in the fort. Here, the important functions of trading, fur grading, and storage were carried on. The Indian House, usually one of the first buildings to be erected at any new fort, was built with an emphasis on security. On entry into the fort, natives would be directed through the Indian yard to the trade room where the

13

Fort Edmonton - 1846

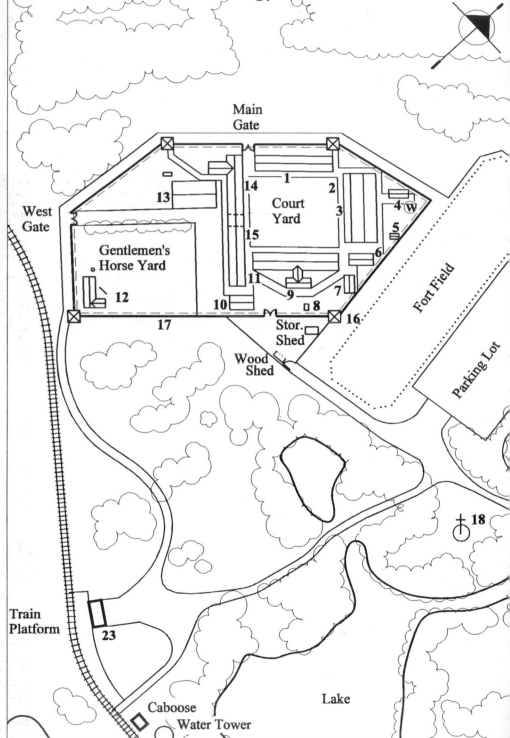

24

Main
Gate

West
Gate

13

14

1

2

3

4 W

Court
Yard

15

5

6

Gentlemen's
Horse Yard

12

11

9

7

10

8

17

16

Stor.
Shed

Wood
Shed

Fort Field

Parking Lot

18

Train
Platform

23

Caboose

Water Tower

Lake

Fort Edmonton - 1846

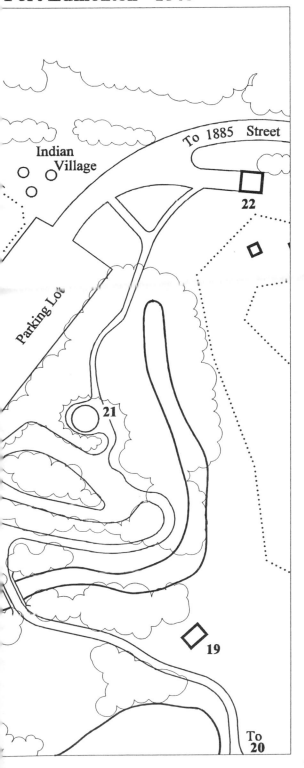

1 Indian House
  a) Indian Room
  b) Trade Store
  c) Fur Loft
2 Fur Press
3 Rowand House
4 Columbia House
5 Watch Tower
6 Meat Store
7 Chapel
8 Bake Oven
9 Clerk's Quarters
10 Ice House
11 Married Men's Quarters
12 Horse Stable
13 Boatshed
14 Blacksmith Shop
15 Tradesmen's Quarters
16 Bastion
17 Pallisades
18 Wooden Cross
19 Metis Cabin
20 Egge's Barn
21 Windmill
22 Trading Post
23 Train Platform
24 York Boat Exhibit

Ⓢ	souvenirs, gifts
Ⓕ	food
Ⓦ	washrooms

furs and other items they had brought with them for trade would be evaluated. Furs accepted in trade would be moved immediately to the fur loft on the second floor, while pemmican, jerky, buffalo tongues and similar food items would be transferred to the meat store.

Once agreement had been reached as to the value of the goods brought in, natives who were known to and trusted by the traders would be allowed, one or two at a time, into the trade store. Others traded through the small wicket in the store wall. The trade store offered items such as cloth, beads, tobacco, blankets, pots, knives, and guns. In the fall, shelves and drawers would be overflowing with goods, but by spring were almost bare.

Next to the store was a storage area for bundles and barrels of extra goods. There was also a small bedroom where an interpreter would sleep during the busy season.

The second floor of the Indian House, called the fur loft, housed the fur processing area. In the spring, the loft was the scene of much activity. The pelts brought in by the natives had to be sorted, graded and baled, all to be ready in time for the departure of the brigades (the groups of men responsible for transporting the furs and goods). The loosely packed bales would be taken to the fur press where they were pressed into smaller, more compact units for transportation.

Rowand House. The entire building, variously called *Rowand House*, the *Big House*, or *Rowand's Folly*, was built for Chief Factor John Rowand in 1832. The house was said to have been the largest structure between Winnipeg and the Rocky Mountains.

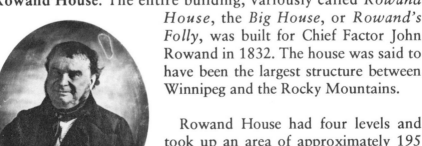

John Rowand

Rowand House had four levels and took up an area of approximately 195 square metres (2100 square feet). The ground floor consisted of storage areas, sleeping quarters, and the kitchen. The steward, the man responsible for overseeing Rowand's servants, had his quarters on the ground floor. As he was also accountable for the liquor supplies, his bedroom was in close proximity to the storage areas. Servants' quarters were located down the hall from his room. Meals

for the people residing in this house, including the Rowand family, other gentlemen, and visitors, were prepared in the large kitchen. A root cellar was located in the northwest corner.

John Rowand's *Big House* in 1871

The main floor included dining rooms, offices, and a large hall. At the top of the stairs leading from the kitchen was a pantry. It was here that the servants divided the food between the large, gentlemen's dining room and the smaller, ladies' dining room. It was customary for women to eat in a separate room, as it was thought that they should not or would not wish to be included in the gentlemen's business discussions. Located just behind the gentlemen's dining room were two offices: John Rowand's was next to the ladies' dining room, while a clerk worked in the other. Next to this office was a bedroom. The remaining large room, known as the *Great Hall*, served a variety of purposes including a meeting room for company officials. From time to time it was also the scene of special ceremonies between native chiefs and John Rowand. As the furs began to pour in during the spring, the Great Hall was also used for the storage of fur bales.

The second floor of Rowand House consisted of the Rowand family's sitting rooms and bedrooms as well as four guest rooms used by gentlemen visitors to the fort such as the Hudson's Bay Company's governor, Sir George Simpson. Chief Trader Harriott had the front bedroom at the north end of the house. In 1846, Rowand, his wife Louise, and daughters Sophia, Margaret, and Adelaide were living in the house. The main sitting room was where the Reverend Robert Rundle provided schooling for the girls. Rowand and Louise shared the first bedroom, Margaret and Adelaide the second bedroom, and Sophia had the corner room to herself.

The remaining level within the Big House was the garret. This large open area was used for storing dried meat which had been processed in the meat house. On the south gable of Rowand House there was a post to which a pulley system was attached for use in hoisting the meat into the garret.

Columbia House was constructed during June and July of 1833. It was built to accommodate the thirty or so men from the Columbia District who arrived annually at Fort Edmonton to join the brigade engaged in transporting furs to York Factory on Hudson Bay. The Columbia District stretched through the Yukon to the Arctic Ocean and south to the northern border of California. The district was bordered on the east by the Rocky Mountains and on the west by the Pacific Ocean. Columbia House was located behind Rowand House and took up an area of 41.9 square metres (450 square feet). The replica of it is currently used as a modern washroom facility.

The Watch Tower afforded a good view of the area outside the fort. From it, the lookout kept an eye on the fort's gardens and livestock. This was necessary, since it appears that theft was a problem in the area. The tower also allowed the lookout to warn the company's men to prepare for incoming traders.

The tower floor is eleven metres (thirty-seven feet) above ground and 0.6 metres (two feet) below the roof line of Rowand House. It was made up of several platforms which were used to construct the walkway on the palisade and to aid in climbing to it. The weather vane on top of the tower is a replica of the one on the original tower.

Meat Store. Dried meat, pemmican, grease, and buffalo tongues were important trade goods at Fort Edmonton. Provisions from Edmonton and the Saskatchewan District supplied all fur brigades (the men responsible for transporting the furs) throughout the company's territories. In addition, provisions were often required from the area for special requirements such as Arctic exploration parties and the military garrison at Red River in the 1840s.

In 1846, the Saskatchewan District supplied some 1,100 bags of pemmican weighing forty-one kilograms (ninety pounds) each, as well as an immense amount of grease, 10,827 kilograms (23,900 pounds) of dried meat, and 6,225 buffalo tongues. Fort Edmonton would have assembled at least one third of this total. The Plains Indians provided much of the meat in their annual trade while hunters from the fort and Métis *freemen* (as opposed to Métis who were company employees) supplied additional amounts. (The Métis were descendants of French traders who married native women.)

The watch tower at the present Fort

The making of pemmican from the meat and grease obtained through trade was an important activity in the fort, especially in the early spring before the brigade left Edmonton. Cutting and melting of fat took place in the kitchens of the fort or on open fires outside when weather permitted. Racks were set up for the drying of meat and dried meat was pounded to a powder in the meat store. With all of the ingredients ready, the actual mixing of the pemmican took place in large wooden troughs. The finished pemmican was put into rawhide bags and stored along with kegs of salted buffalo tongues and other related provisions in the meat store. The tongues were sent to England where they were considered to be a great delicacy.

Rundle Chapel. The Reverend Robert Terrill Rundle, a missionary sent out to the Saskatchewan District by the Wesleyan Methodist

Reverend Robert Rundle

Church in 1840, was provided with a chapel built in 1843. It was described as a convenient house of three rooms: two small rooms for Rundle's private use and a larger one which served as the chapel. The furnishings were simple and few.

The Clerks' Quarters housed all the single men living at the fort. Before the completion of the Big House, Rowand and his family resided in this building which could possibly explain why this structure had glass windows instead of the more usual parchment.

The original clerks' quarters was a two story structure. The main floor contained a kitchen, a large dining area and two smaller rooms at each end. These two rooms were used as offices and sleeping areas for the fort's clerks. The kitchen included a large fireplace and food preparation area as well as sleeping quarters for the cook and his family. The dining hall was where the 20 to 30 bachelors, including clerks, interpreters, servants, old men, and transient hunters, ate their meals. It was here that fort festivities such as Christmas, New Year, and brigade arrival celebrations were held. The artist Paul Kane, in his book *Wanderings of an Artist Among the Indians of North America,* described the Christmas dinner which took place there in 1847 during his visit to Fort Edmonton.

The second floor garret, divided into a number of smaller rooms, was first used as living quarters for the Rowand family. When Rowand moved into the Big House, these rooms became bedrooms for the bachelors living at the fort.

Bake Oven. The outdoor bake oven, a common feature of Hudson's Bay Company posts, was located just outside the clerks' quarters' kitchen. As it was next to impossible to transport large metal ovens by York boat, the inhabitants were compelled to make their own ovens, in most cases using materials found locally. First, a platform was constructed on which the base of the oven was laid. The base consisted of a layer of clay and rock. The domed oven roof was made by covering a willow branch frame with clay and mud. A small opening in the oven roof served as a flue. A second opening was used as the oven door.

Baking bread required lighting a wood fire inside the oven and letting it burn for about forty-five minutes. Once the oven was heated, the remaining coals and embers were scraped out and the oven floor mopped. Next bread dough was placed in the oven using

Fort Edmonton in 1890

a long wooden paddle called a *peel* (possibly from the French *pelle* meaning *shovel,* which the paddle closely resembled). The wooden door of the oven was then sealed tightly with clay. After forty-five to sixty minutes, the bread was baked. The oven was used throughout the year, although in very cold weather, it might take as long as two hours to heat.

Ice House. The storage of perishable goods such as fresh meat posed an obvious problem for the fort's inhabitants. To solve this, ice houses were constructed to store meat for summer consumption. Artist Paul Kane, a visitor to the fort during the winter of 1847-48, described the construction of an ice house as follows.

"The men had already commenced gathering their supply of fresh meat for the summer in the ice pit. This is made by digging a square hole, capable of containing 700 or 800 carcasses. As soon as the ice in the river is of significant thickness, it is cut into square blocks of uniform size with saws; with these blocks the floor of the pit is regularly paved, and blocks cemented together by pouring water between them, and allowing it to freeze solid. In like manner, the

walls are built up to the level of the ground. The head and feet of the buffalo, when killed, are cut off, and the carcass, without being skinned, is divided into quarters, and piled in layers

View of the Fort in 1910 looking to the south

in the pit as brought in, until it is filled up. Then the hole is covered with a thick coating of straw, which is again protected from the sun and rain by a shed. In this manner, the meat keeps perfectly good through the whole summer and eats much better than fresh killed meat, being more tender and better flavoured." (from *Wanderings of an Artist Among the Indians of North America.*)

The ice house, built over the pit, was of special construction. It was usually built with double walls about 0.3 metres (one foot) apart, the space being filled with earth as insulation. A sod roof provided protection from the sun. The pit itself, generally about six metres (twenty feet) deep and three metres (ten feet) by six metres at the top, was separated by a wall from the work area where meat was weighed and cut, and daily rations distributed. After two or three years, the ice house was moved and placed over a new pit, as the smell, due to rotting meat left at the bottom of the pit, became overpowering.

Married Men's and Tradesmen's Quarters. These quarters housed the servants, tradesmen, labourers, and their families. The eight large units were usually crowded as each unit housed two or three families. All units were under the same long roof with each unit having a living area with a loft and a cellar. The furnishings were handmade. Illumination was by fire or, occasionally, tallow candles. The open area just behind the married men's quarters was used to harness the dog teams.

The shops and living quarters of the carpenter, cooper, and blacksmith were located in the same building. The carpenter built the various buildings or supervised their construction. He also made furniture, repaired most wooden items, and manufactured agricultural tools. The cooper manufactured the many barrels, kegs, buckets, and tubs needed in the fort. The blacksmith's shop contained work benches, bellows, a forge, and tools for making and repairing the different metal items which the fort required.

The York boat builder had a shed behind his quarters. This was a simple roofed shed with the sides left open for accessibility. In the same area there was a steam trough (for bending pieces of wood) and a sawing platform.

The Horse Yard and Gentlemen's Stable were used mainly by the gentlemen of the fort, who kept their animals close at hand. Cattle were kept here as well. The yard and stable were located inside the fort palisades in order to protect the horses from theft. Horses received in trade from the natives were also kept in this yard for a few weeks to ensure that they would not attempt to return to their original owners.

The York Boat was a major means of river transportation used by the Hudson's Bay Company from 1749 until the early years of the twentieth century. The York boat, named for the Hudson's Bay Company's York Factory, refers to an inland boat with long, pointed ends, closely resembling the fishing boats of the Orkney Islands off the coast of Scotland. It was the men of the Orkneys who were usually recruited to build them for the Hudson's Bay Company. George Sutherland constructed the first York boat built at the original Edmonton House in 1795. York boats constructed at Fort Edmonton usually had an 8.5 metre (28 foot) keel. Even when carrying fifty to seventy, forty-one kilogram bales (over 2,700 kilograms), the boats drew only 0.6 metres (two feet) of water.

While the York boats could carry twice as much as the smaller freight canoes (with the same number of crewmen), carrying them over a portage involved heavy labour. Roads three metres (ten feet) wide had to be cut through the woods, and roller logs laid 0.9 metres (three feet) apart along this road. In addition, the crew of six to eight men had to unload the boat and carry its cargo over these portages. Since they were constructed of soft wood, the lifespan of a York boat was usually no more than three years. Planks, nails, and pitch were always taken along on a voyage to handle unexpected repairs.

York boats on Lake Winnipeg

The boat shed at Fort Edmonton has constructed replicas of the York boat for the Park's displays.

Indian Camp. While the tipis at Fort Edmonton represent the dwellings of the Cree people during the fur trade period, the area around what is now Edmonton was originally inhabited by the Beaver, the Sarsi, and to the south, the Blackfoot. These are the tribes who met the first explorers in the region. The Cree people gradually began to move westward from Saskatchewan into the Edmonton region after 1760, some thirty years before the fur trading posts were established along the North Saskatchewan River.

Windmill. The 1840s marked a period of increased demand on the

24

food supplies of the Red River region, partly owing to the presence of a British garrison in the colony for two years. In order to help relieve some of this pressure, Edmonton was expected to provide not only more dried meat and grease, but horses, horned cattle, and flour as well. The construction of a mill at Edmonton by the Hudson's Bay Company was supposed to lessen the dependance of the brigades and northern districts on Red River-grown grain. On the fields around the fort, labourers planted crops of wheat, barley, and oats for milling.

The windmill is a replica of the original which was built in 1846 and stood on the hill above the fort, approximately on the site of the present Alberta legislature. The mill is a *cap* or *smock* type, measuring 15.5 metres (fifty-one feet) high and 7.3 metres (twenty-four feet) in diameter at its base. In this type of mill, the cap rotates a full 360 degrees, allowing the sails to catch the wind from any direction.

There were many millers at Fort Edmonton during the mill's life. William Bird built the mill and operated it off and on from about 1846. Other millers included Thomas Hudson (or Hodgeson), Thomas Cameron, Angus MacLeod, and William Flett. Sometime between October 1866 and December 1867 an animal-powered mill replaced the old structure.

From 1847 to 1866, the windmill produced flour for

The Windmill at Fort Edmonton Park

the brigades and Northern Districts as well as the fort itself. While mills were erected in other parts of the prairies, only those in the Edmonton area and at the Red River Settlement in what was later to become Manitoba had a major impact on the agriculture of the area surrounding them.

Trading Post. While the trading post located between the fur fort and 1885 Street is not based on any historical prototype, it serves a useful modern-day function for visitors to the Park. Tickets for the wagon, stage coach, and pony rides may be purchased here as well as souvenirs, film, postcards, soda pop, snacks, native craft items and jewellery. For the convenience of visitors, there is a public pay telephone on the post's rear wall.

Cross of the First Missionaries. In the fall of 1838, the first missionaries in Alberta, Father Norbert Blanchet and Father Modeste Demers, arrived by canoe at Fort Edmonton. Before they left for the West Coast on September 10 of the same year, they erected a cross on the crest of the hill overlooking the fort. The base of the cross eventually decayed, and a new cross was raised by Father Lacombe in 1883.

The present cross, erected south of the fort, is a replica of the first cross. It commemorates the visit of Pope John Paul II to Edmonton on September 17 and 18, 1984. Blessed by him during his stay in Edmonton, it is a spiritual and historical tribute to the Catholic missionary heritage of Western Canada.

Métis Cabin. The Métis are the descendants of the marriages between native women and European traders.

Until about 1868, the Métis built temporary villages where they lived during the winter. In the summer they lived in tents or tipis as they moved out onto the plains in search of the buffalo. By the end of the 1870s, however, permanent settlements were being constructed, and many of the Métis began to earn their living by farming, freight hauling, and ranching. The Métis in Alberta, most of whom were French-speaking and Catholic, settled mainly in St. Albert, Lac La Biche, and Lac Ste Anne. The church established missions at St. Albert and Lac Ste Anne, the latter as early as 1840.

The Métis cabin at Fort Edmonton Park is typical of the dwellings to be found in these more permanent settlements.

The lake and creek system reproduced at Fort Edmonton Park has its origins in Edmonton's early history. In the mid-1800s, the Hudson's Bay Company used the pasture surrounding McKernan's Lake (on 76 Avenue at about 116 Street) as grazing land for its pack horses. Many years after the pack trains to Rocky Mountain House and Tête Jaune Cache passed into history, Edmontonians enjoyed winter skating on this lake. Long since drained and developed, no trace of McKernan's Lake remains.

Part of the lake and creek system

Unlike the landscaped water systems common in large city parks, the Park's lake and creek system is typical of the slough and marsh lands of Northern Alberta. As a result, it has become a natural wildlife sanctuary that is attracting ever increasing numbers of migratory birds. The nearby woodland is home to many deer.

The creek is approximately 137 metres (450 feet) long and the lake covers in excess of 186 square metres (2,000 square feet). Through the use of pumps, its water is re-circulated drawing only a minimal amount from the North Saskatchewan River.

The Red River cart carried much of the merchandise arriving in Edmonton from Winnipeg over the Carlton Trail from the 1840s to the 1890s. The cart was made up of a light box mounted on a single pair of wheels 1.5 to 1.8 metres (five to six feet) in diameter. The materials used in its construction were usually wood and buffalo hide, items generally available in most parts of the prairies. The axles were not greased, since the dust along the trail would have mixed with the grease to freeze the axles. The result was a hideous squealing of wheel and axle which could be heard for some distance. The carts were usually pulled by a single horse or ox, and averaged about eight kilometres (five miles) a day.

Métis buffalo hunters also used the vehicles to carry the carcases of the animals back to their settlements.

A Red River Cart and its driver

1885 STREET - SETTLEMENT ERA (1871-1891)

The buildings located on 1885 Street represent the community of Edmonton gradually being established outside the walls of the Hudson's Bay Company fort. Since the town was still in its settlement stage, most of these establishments were developed in response to the needs of daily living. The blacksmith, the doctor, the harness maker, the hardware merchant, even the church and the school are all included in this category, as are most of the businesses on 1885 street. When Edmonton was incorporated as a town in 1892, its population still numbered only some 700 persons.

Despite its small population, the Edmonton of the settlement era was not limited to one business of each type. Several hotels flourished in Edmonton in the 1880s, just as there were several blacksmiths, and several harness makers. At the Park, however, 1885 Street offers a single example of each type of business or service as it existed in the days before the coming of the railway.

Jasper Avenue in 1890

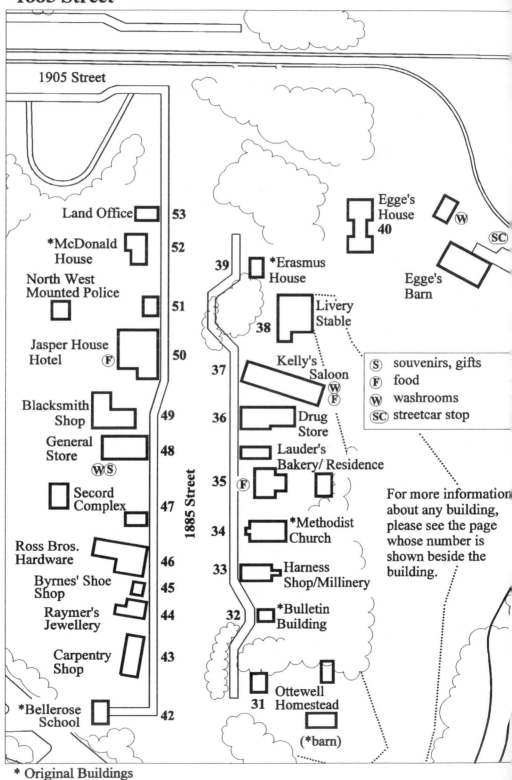

1885 Street

1905 Street

Land Office 53

*McDonald House 52

North West Mounted Police 51

Jasper House Hotel Ⓕ 50

Blacksmith Shop 49

General Store 48

ⓌⓈ

Secord Complex 47

Ross Bros. Hardware 46

Byrnes' Shoe Shop 45

Raymer's Jewellery 44

Carpentry Shop 43

*Bellerose School 42

1885 Street

39 *Erasmus House

38 Livery Stable

37 Kelly's Saloon ⓌⒻ

36 Drug Store

Lauder's Bakery/Residence

35 Ⓕ

34 *Methodist Church

33 Harness Shop/Millinery

32 *Bulletin Building

31 Ottewell Homestead

(*barn)

Egge's House 40 Ⓦ

ⓈⒸ

Egge's Barn

Ⓢ souvenirs, gifts
Ⓕ food
Ⓦ washrooms
ⓈⒸ streetcar stop

For more information about any building, please see the page whose number is shown beside the building.

* Original Buildings

THE OTTEWELL HOMESTEAD was located in the Clover Bar area east of Edmonton and south of the North Saskatchewan River. While the house is a replica, the barn is an original structure from the same era, although not from the Ottewell homestead. The chicken coop, turkey shed, and piggery, all replicas, reflect the homestead's effort to be self-sufficient.

Born in England in 1848, Richard Ottewell emigrated to Port Arthur, Ontario (now Thunder Bay), where in 1877 he married Frances Trevillion. Leaving his family, he set out for Edmonton in 1881 and in early August became a squatter on the site described above until such time as the area was surveyed and he could obtain title. For the first winter Ottewell lived in a sod-roofed dugout. In the spring of 1882 he began to clear and break land and managed to harvest a small

The Ottewell home on 1885 Street

crop of barley. In July 1883 he was able to file for his original claim and pre-empt another quarter section. That fall, after the harvest was complete, he returned east to bring his family back to their new home. The house was constructed in the fall of 1884.

Ottewell was not only a farmer. He purchased a steam threshing outfit and threshed for nearby farmers. In 1904 he opened the Ottewell Coal Mine and bought an interest in two local flour mills. Later, he switched from mixed farming to dairy farming.

The Ottewells had six boys and three girls all of whom were raised in the log house. Later, Ottewell was able to construct a fifteen-room, brick house more suitable for the family's needs. He died in 1942 at the age of 93. His sons continued to farm the site until 1951 when most of the land was sold to provide space for the beginning of Edmonton's industrial growth. The Canadian Celanese plant now stands on the site of Ottewell's farm.

THE *BULLETIN* BUILDING, one of the oldest surviving structures in Edmonton, is the original dovetailed log building constructed by

Frank Oliver

Frank Oliver in 1878 on the south side of Jasper Avenue between Queens Avenue (99 Street) and McDougall Avenue (100 Street). Oliver first used the building as a general store, with his living quarters upstairs. By 1880 it had become the office of Edmonton's first newspaper, *The Bulletin.*

Oliver was born in Ontario in 1853. In 1873 he moved to Winnipeg where he worked as a printer on the *Winnipeg Free Press.* Oliver left Winnipeg in 1876, arriving in Edmonton in 1877. He became one of the small traders in the area, and for the next three years ran freight between Winnipeg and Edmonton. In 1881 he married Harriet Dunlop, daughter of Thomas Dunlop of Prairie Grove, Manitoba.

In 1880, Oliver purchased a small printing press on which he published the first issue of *The Bulletin* on December 6, 1880. From its earliest days, the little paper concentrated on subjects affecting the development of Edmonton. Emphasizing that solutions to western problems must originate in the west, *The Bulletin* soon became the voice of the Northwest.

Oliver was a member of the North-West Council from 1883 to 1885, and was twice elected to the Legislative Assembly of the North-West Territories. In 1896 he was elected to the House of Commons in Ottawa serving until 1917. From 1905 to 1911 he acted as minister of the interior and from 1923 to 1928 as the Federal government's railway commissioner. When the province of Alberta was formed in 1905, Oliver was instrumental in having Edmonton selected as the provincial capital. He died on March 31, 1933.

Bulletin Building — Canadian Imperial Bank of Commerce

KERNOHAN'S MILLINERY SHOP AND HUTCHINGS AND RILEY'S HARNESS SHOP recreate the original building constructed in 1888 on the north side of Jasper Avenue between Queens Avenue (99 Street) and McDougall Avenue (100 Street). The structure originally housed only Mrs. Kernohan's business.

Hutchings and Riley's harness shop did not open on the main floor until 1891. Since horses were the principal means of transportation in Edmonton at the time, harness making was a profitable business. The harness maker also sold blankets, saddles, curry combs and brushes, muzzles, harness soaps and oils, assorted horse salves and remedies, and even axle oils and greases. The firm's manager, H. A. Finch, purchased the business in February, 1893.

James and Mary Elizabeth Kernohan and their two children, Frank and Lulu, originally settled on a homestead in north Edmonton prior to 1886. Kernohan supplemented his homesteading by hauling freight from Calgary. Mrs. Kernohan opened her store just before Christmas in 1888. Her business included not only millinery, but also stationery, ladies' and girls' apparel, and a few fancy foodstuffs. It closed temporarily in late 1890, but re-opened again in April 1891, this time occupying just the top floor and then only until July 25 of the same year when it closed for the last time. The space was then occupied by Dr. Braithwaite until 1893.

The harness shop after Finch took over

33

THE METHODIST CHURCH, completed in 1873, was one of the first buildings constructed outside the walls of Fort Edmonton. The log church, built by George McDougall, John Walter, and some

of the Hudson's Bay Company employees, was built facing the river on land owned by the Methodist church. It was replaced in 1892 by a new Methodist church at 10025-101 Street, site of the present McDougall United Church. The log church was then moved to the site of the present *Edmonton Journal* building. About 1904, it was moved again to Alberta College on the east side of 101 Street where it was used as a boys' dormitory until 1920 when it became a store-house. Restoration of the building as an historic site was completed in 1946, and in 1978 it was moved to Fort Edmonton Park.

Reverend George McDougall

George McDougall was born in 1821 at Kingston, Ontario. In 1842, he married Elizabeth Chantler and spent the first six years of married life farming near Owen Sound.

McDougall and his son John entered the Methodist ministry and established missions, first among the native people in Alberta and later in Ontario. In 1860 McDougall was appointed to the mission at Norway House in Manitoba. Later, he moved his family to Victoria (now Pakan), Alberta. In 1871 McDougall moved to Edmonton, leaving John in charge of the mission at Victoria.

The McDougalls remained in Edmonton until 1873 when they left for Morleyville (now called Morley), on the Bow River west of Calgary. McDougall died tragically in a blizzard there in January, 1876. He is buried in the mission cemetery at Morley.

LAUDER'S BAKERY AND RESIDENCE recall the buildings on

Fraser Avenue (98 Street) where James Lauder began his bakery business in November 1885. The residence he built beside the bakery included a store where the Lauders sold confectionery, baked goods, fruit, and vegetables. The family owned the home from 1886 to 1896 after which it was used for the offices of Dr. McInnis and Dr. Wilson. The house was later used for different businesses including a restaurant, a shoe repair store, and in the 1920s, a laundry.

James Lauder

Born in Scotland in 1843, James Lauder married Hannah Gray in 1862 and emigrated to Canada in 1874. He settled in Winnipeg, and his wife and eight children arrived shortly after. On moving to Edmonton in 1881, he built a house and a hotel, Lauderdale House. A few years later, Lauder sold the hotel and took up a homestead in what is now Edmonton's Lauderdale district.

Even before establishing his bakery business, Lauder held a contract to bake bread for the NWMP. Soon he was also baking for the St. Albert Mission and the Hudson's Bay Company. Lauder's son Thomas managed the business, while his father did the baking. When Lauder suffered a stroke in 1897, his wife and daughter-in-law tried to continue, but eventually had to sell the firm.

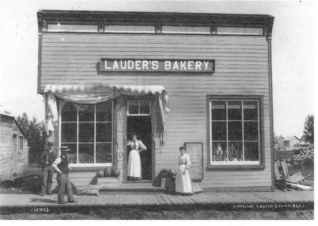

The Lauders in front of the bakery

DALY'S DRUGSTORE AND DR. WILSON'S OFFICE were located

Philip Daly

in a building constructed in 1882 for Dr. Herbert Wilson by James McDonald at the corner of Fifth Street (105 Street) and McKay Avenue (99 Avenue). Dr. Wilson operated the drugstore downstairs and practiced medicine in the upstairs rooms. The arrangement proved inconvenient, and in 1883 offices were built for the doctor at the rear of the building. He kept his residence upstairs. In 1886 Philip Daly bought out the doctor's supply of drugs and rented the front of the building.

An advertisement for the store printed in 1887 lists sale items ranging from toys to potato mashers to groceries and fancy foods. Daly's may therefore be thought of as the forerunner of the modern drugstore. Since Daly had brought a large iron safe with him from Winnipeg he also became the town's first banker, a function which ceased as more conventional banks opened in the community. The drugstore's business was so good that Daly opened a branch store in the centre of town. In 1890 Daly sold his drug business and went into the flour and feed business.

Dr. Herbert Wilson was born in 1859 at Picton, Ontario. He graduated both as a pharmacist and as a medical doctor. Wilson practiced medicine in Toronto for one year before moving to Edmonton in 1882 where he became Edmonton's third physician. He married Emily Lee of Toronto.

Dr. Herbert Wilson

He was elected to the North-West Territories Council in 1885. When the council was abolished in 1888, and the new legislative assembly for the territories established, Dr. Wilson became a member and its first speaker. In 1895 he was elected mayor of Edmonton for one term.

KELLY'S SALOON was located on the northeast corner of Fraser Avenue (98 Street) and Jasper Avenue. The business, which opened on August 24, 1883, contained a saloon and billiard hall

on the main floor and a public hall upstairs. In 1885, a restaurant was added at the rear of the building. The following year the second story was rebuilt as hotel rooms, and the restaurant incorporated into a two-story addition. The structure then became the Alberta Hotel. In 1892 Kelly leased the hotel to Frank Mariaggi who bought it outright in 1895. In 1903 Mariaggi built a new brick structure, also called the Alberta Hotel, on the same site.

Eliza Pagorio   Luke Kelly was born in Ontario in 1854. He became a shoemaker and when he came to Edmonton, he built a combined shoe store and residence in 1881 on Jasper Avenue at Namayo Avenue (97 Street). He also opened his first saloon the same year. By 1883 the premises proved to be inadequate, and Kelly then built the second saloon described above. At the same time he sold his shoemaking business to Patrick Byrnes.

Kelly brought his mother, brother, and sisters to Edmonton in 1893 along with equipment for a billiard room and twenty gallons of illegal liquor. Prohibition in Edmonton was especially hard on the hotel owners and saloon keepers.

In 1896 Kelly married Eliza Pagerie, reputed to be the best cook in the area. The couple had five children.

The first Alberta Hotel

McCAULEY'S LIVERY STABLE stood on the site of the present McCauley Plaza, on Jasper Avenue between McDougall Avenue (100 Street) and First Street (101 Street). In pre-automobile days, the livery stable was an important business. It could provide the traveller with horses, rigs, and even drivers. The livery stable was the pioneer equivalent of both the taxi company and the car rental agency. Some also sold feed, livestock, and farm machinery.

Matthew (Matt) McCauley was born in Ontario in 1850 and

farmed in the Owen Sound area until coming west in 1871. He worked at Fort Garry as a labourer until 1874, then went into the teaming, draying, and hack business. In 1879 he moved to Fort Saskatchewan and opened his first livery stable before coming to

McCauley's livery stable on 1885 Street

Edmonton to establish a livery stable here in 1881. In 1889 he sold a half interest to W. G. Ibbotson, and the firm eventually became the Edmonton Cartage Company. In 1902 McCauley sold his share.

In 1875 McCauley married Matilda Benson with whom he had eight children. Matilda died in 1896, and in 1906 McCauley married Annie Cookson with whom he had four more children.

McCauley, who had worked hard to bring Edmonton to town status, was elected the town's first mayor, serving from 1892 to 1895. Active in many organizations, he was instrumental in the establishment of the Edmonton School District, serving as its chairman from 1881 to 1888, and as a member of the board in the mid-1890s. From 1896 to 1903 he was elected Liberal member of the Territorial Council for the District of Vermilion. In 1906 he was appointed warden of the Federal Penitentiary at Edmonton, a post which he held until 1911.

PETER ERASMUS HOUSE was originally located four kilometres (two and one-half miles) west of Pakan (formerly Victoria) on the Victoria Trail. Before being brought to Fort Edmonton Park it formed part of the Great North-West Pioneer Village (no longer in operation) on Highway 16. James Erasmus (a son) and his family lived in the house until 1941.

Erasmus, whose father was Danish and whose mother was native, was born in the Red River settlement at Kildonan, Manitoba in 1833, the fourth of six children. In 1852 he entered St. John's College in Winnipeg, but three years later left to become a guide and interpreter for the Reverend Thomas Woolsey, a Methodist missionary. He filled the same role with the Palliser Expedition in 1858. In 1861 he moved to Whitefish Lake where he built a log cabin and married Charlotte. For the next few years he again acted as a guide and interpreter, this time for Reverend George McDougall who was visiting Victoria, Edmonton, and other western native settlements.

The couple had six children, four boys and two girls: Eliza, James, Robert, Caroline, David, and George. Two years after Charlotte's death in 1880, Erasmus married Mary Stanley of Whitefish Lake with whom he had three more children, all girls: Sarah, Lily, and Catherine. It was this second family that lived in the house which is now in Fort Edmonton Park.

Erasmus was unusual in that along with an extensive knowledge and appreciation of the Cree language and culture, he had received a good education and was fluent in both English and French. As a result, he was one of the finest interpreters in the West. He was present at the signing of Treaty No. 6 which involved central Alberta and central Saskatchewan.

Peter Erasmus

39

EGGE'S STOPPING HOUSE, located on the Athabasca Trail near Halfway Lake and Clyde, 45 miles north of Edmonton, included a

house in which the post office and the telegraph station for the area were located. A large barn, Pennsylvania Dutch in style, accommodated twenty-five to thirty teams of horses. Two smaller barns, a granary, a wagon shed, an ice house, and a bunkhouse for the teamsters who hauled freight along the trail also formed part of the site. At Fort Edmonton Park, the bunkhouse has been modified to serve as washrooms. The front half of the house is the original structure.

The Egges

The stopping house was an important institution along the major travel routes of Western Canada. It was basically a farm house which took in guests for a fixed price. Meals were provided at extra cost. In the nineteenth century, the provision of hay and shelter for the horses was a primary concern, perhaps even more so than food and shelter for the traveller. The rates charged at similar stopping houses may be of interest. Fifty cents usually provided hay and shelter overnight for a team of horses, and additional hay could be provided at noon for a further fifteen cents.

Newton Egge was born in Wisconsin or Iowa in 1853, later moving with his family to the North Central States where he married his wife Cynthia about 1887. Egge himself then moved to Edmonton in

Egge's stopping house at the Park

Travellers at Egge's Stopping House

1894, and the rest of the family followed within a year. The couple had four sons and two daughters.

For the first three or four years, Egge worked as a coal miner. He then established a homestead on the Athabasca Trail which was a busy and important land route linking Edmonton to the north via the Mackenzie River system. The homestead became a stopping house in 1903 or 1904. Later, when the railway arrived in the area, there was no further business for the stopping house. The Egges continued farming on the site until 1917 when they moved to Montana.

THE BELLEROSE SCHOOL, built in 1886, was originally located on the homestead of Octave Bellerose on the north side of the Sturgeon River beside the road which connected St. Albert and Namao. Its pupils, most of whom were of French descent, came from a wide area. The upper floor was first used as living quarters in 1894 by the school's third teacher, Victoria LePage, who came west from Rimouski, Québec, in 1889.

Bellerose School

Early teachers, in addition to Mlle LePage, included Alfred Arcand, a former North-West Mounted Police officer, who took up farming next to the Bellerose homestead. He became the school's first teacher from 1885 to 1888. Until the school was built, classes were held in his home. The second teacher, George W. Gairdner, taught in the school beginning in 1888. In addition to his teaching duties, Gairdner was a farmer and a justice of the peace.

The log building was last used as a school in 1947 by the Roman Catholic Public School District No. 6 in the Sturgeon School Division.

JAMES McDONALD'S CARPENTRY SHOP originally stood on

McDonald's carpentry shop

Jasper Avenue at Queens Avenue (99 Street).

McDonald was born in Scotland in 1846 and emigrated to Canada as a young boy. He moved to Winnipeg in 1874 where he married Caroline Robertson. Five years later, in 1879, the couple moved to Edmonton. A respected carpenter and cabinet maker, he soon gained a reputation as a builder and contractor. The *Bulletin* building and Daly's drug store are two of the commercial buildings he constructed in Edmonton. He also built a number of fine homes.

McDonald was a school trustee and a founding member of the Board of Trade. A public-spirited man, he taught school free of charge in 1881, since regular schools had not yet been established. He was a member of the Edmonton Literary Club, the Edmonton Rifle Club, and the Masons, and also helped to form a skating and curling club.

In the late 1890s, McDonald started a company which dealt in real estate and sold other commodities - fire, accident, and plate glass insurance, Newcombe pianos, and Goldie and McCulloch safes.

James McDonald

43

RAYMER'S JEWELLERY STORE was constructed some time before the fall of 1880 on the corner of Queens Avenue (99 Street) and Jasper Avenue. It is believed to have been the first frame building in Edmonton outside the fort. Emmanuel Raymer moved into the building in 1888.

Little is known about his early life other than that he was employed in 1885 in Portage la Prairie, Manitoba by the jewellery firm of McIntyre and Davidson. In 1886 Raymer came to Edmonton as their agent, setting up his wares in the Jasper House hotel as was the practice of salesmen at the time. He decided to remain in Edmonton and established his own jewellery business. Despite the heavy competition from travelling salesmen and from stores operated by John McDougall and the Hudson's Bay Company, Raymer succeeded because he also offered watch and jewellery repair. In later years he added books, eye glasses, magazines, and stationery to his stock. For a time he acted as agent for the Portage la Prairie Marble Works.

Emmanuel Raymer

A talented singer and accomplished guitar player, Raymer helped to found the Edmonton Glee Club in 1887 and took part in many of the club's productions. He was active in the business community and was a charter member of the Edmonton Board of Trade. In 1899, along with others, he organized the prestigious Edmonton Club. On his retirement in 1906, Raymer sold his business to the Jackson brothers and left the Edmonton area.

Raymer's jewellery store is shown in the photograph on the following page.

BYRNES' SHOE SHOP. Patrick Byrnes was born in Ireland in 1844. He emigrated to the United States in 1867 settling in Philadelphia where he lived until 1882. He then moved to Winnipeg where he met Luke Kelly who persuaded him to come to Edmonton. They arrived in the city on July 13, 1883, and one month later Byrnes set up as a shoemaker in a small building owned by Kelly directly behind Kelly and McLeod's Billiard Hall on Fraser Avenue (98 Street). By May 1884, Kelly and McLeod had decided to construct an addition at the rear of their billiard hall, and it was then that Byrnes purchased the west half of the Ross brothers' lot on Main Street (Jasper Avenue east) and moved the little shop to it.

A bachelor all his life, Byrnes returned from a visit to Rainy River, Ontario in 1885 with six green canaries. Apart from the canaries and his work, Byrnes seems to have had few other interests. Over the years he purchased several lots on Jasper Avenue. Edmonton was growing rapidly, and, by the time of his death in 1917, the lots were worth several hundred thousand dollars.

Raymer's Jewellery and Byrnes' Shoe Store 1890

ROSS BROTHERS' HARDWARE was constructed in 1884. The structure in Fort Edmonton Park represents its appearance between 1886 and 1890 at Jasper Avenue and Fraser Avenue (98 Street). The main part of the building housed the hardware store, while the rear annex contained the tinsmithing shop. The business did very well, and the company grew from a small tinsmith shop to the largest wholesale and retail hardware business in western Canada. The building was demolished in 1911.

James "Charlie" Ross (1851 - 1936) was born in Toronto where he worked for some time as a fireman on the Grand Trunk Railway. He apprenticed as a tinsmith in Winnipeg from 1874 until 1879 when he came to Edmonton and found employment as a carpenter and a freighter. In 1882 he returned to tinsmithing and established a hardware business with his brother in 1883. Charlie Ross was active in the cultural activities of the community, was a member of the Board of Trade, and served four terms as an alderman. He married Helen McBeath in 1888. The couple had three children.

Ross Brothers' Hardware in 1890

Frederick "Fred" Ross (1863 - 1949) was born in Toronto. He worked both there and in Winnipeg as a tinsmith before coming to Edmonton in 1883 to join his brother in business. He was a Mason (as was his brother) and served on the Board of Trade for several years. Fred was the *entrepreneur* in the family, and as long as he and Charlie remained in business together, it was Fred who was the president. Upon his retirement the firm was sold to Marshall Wells. Fred Ross married Lucy Kennedy in 1897. The couple had one daughter.

THE SECORD FUR STORE AND WAREHOUSE are replicas of the

original buildings built by Richard Secord in 1887. In 1890, these structures were moved to a site on the north side of Jasper Avenue between First and Second Streets (101 and 102 Streets), where they remained until 1915.

The original fur store and warehouse

The store was not a store in the strict sense, as nothing was sold there. Instead, it was used to receive furs, and the warehouse behind it served as an area for grading and packing furs and for storage. Trappers came to the store to have their furs evaluated, receiving immediate cash in return. Consequently, it also became a meeting place for the trappers. The Secord Fur Store and Warehouse represent the transition from the Hudson's Bay Company's monopoly on fur trading to an era when private traders became serious competitors in the business.

Secord, who was born in 1860 in Ontario, arrived in Edmonton in September, 1881. He first worked on the crew surveying the river lots of the Edmonton Settlement. In 1883, he took up teaching, first at a school for native children at Victoria (now Pakan, Alberta), and later at Edmonton's MacKay Avenue School. When he retired from teaching, he worked for a short while as a clerk in McDougall's Store. In June, 1888, he opened a fur buying store at Athabasca Landing.

Secord married Annie York in 1891, and they had four children. He was well respected in the community and was elected Conservative member of the North-West Territories for Edmonton. He was also one of the original backers of the *Edmonton Journal*.

Annie Secord

J. A. McDOUGALL'S GENERAL STORE stood at the corner of Fraser Avenue (98 Street) and Jasper Avenue. John Alexander McDougall was born in Ontario in 1854. In 1874 he went to Winnipeg and for a short time worked in a fur store owned by the Henderson who founded Henderson's city directories. He left

Winnipeg in 1875 and, while in Prince Albert, Saskatchewan, met Frank Oliver. In 1878 he married Lovisa Amey. The couple arrived in Edmonton in 1879. They had five children - Edmund, James, John, Alice, and Annie.

The McDougall Store

With financial backing from a Winnipeg firm, McDougall set up a store which was the first serious rival in the area to the Hudson's Bay Company. In 1883 he moved into the building whose replica stands on 1885 Street in Fort Edmonton Park.

McDougall's talents were in great demand. At one time he was auditor for the Agricultural Society, active on the management committees for both the Methodist and Presbyterian churches, and because of his excellent penmanship, the secretary at many meetings. In 1881 he was one of the ten original guarantors of the first teacher's salary, and in 1889 the driving force behind the first Board of Trade. In 1897 and again in 1908 he served as Edmonton's mayor.

J. A. McDougall

48

SANDERSON AND LOOBY, BLACKSMITHS. The replica of this shop built in 1881 on the northwest corner of Namayo Avenue (97 Street) and Jasper Avenue is divided into four sections: blacksmith shop, carriage repair shop, the Sanderson residence, and the bunk loft.

Sanderson and Looby at their shop

By 1889 when the town's population numbered about 700 persons, there were five blacksmith shops in or near Edmonton. The blacksmith's most common task was to shoe horses, but he also fashioned wrought iron into hinges, latches, hooks, and other similar items. His work often included harness and carriage-making.

George Pringle Sanderson (1850-1940) was born in Ontario but went to Winnipeg in 1877 where he worked as a blacksmith before coming to Edmonton in 1881. After successfully opening Edmonton's second blacksmith shop (the first was in the fort), he returned to Winnipeg where he married Julia Simpson. The Sandersons had three children.

After returning to Edmonton, Sanderson took an active role in several community organizations including serving as Edmonton's first fire chief. As time went on he spent less time blacksmithing and started to work on bicycles. He was also an excellent locksmith.

Edward Looby (1855-1914), also born in Ontario, moved to Winnipeg in 1879. In 1881 he came to Edmonton with Sanderson, working at first as a teamster. As partners, Sanderson was the black-smith and farrier, Looby the harnessmaker and wheelwright.

The pair operated the blacksmith business until 1887. After that Looby continued the business alone in the original building which later became known as the City Harness Shop.

THE JASPER HOUSE HOTEL is a replica of the original hotel built in 1882 which is still operating at 9692 Jasper Avenue as the Hub Hotel. The Hub Hotel is probably the oldest surviving building in Edmonton still used for commercial purposes.

Built by James Goodridge, the Jasper House hotel was the first brick-veneered building in Edmonton. The hotel contained a small kitchen, a dining room, an office, a saloon and a lounge on the main floor, with guest rooms and the Goodridge's living quarters on the second floor. Goodridge must have enjoyed success, since in 1884 he constructed a large addition to the building. The balcony was not added until 1896. The Jasper House hotel also functioned as the office and terminus of the Edmonton to Calgary stage line.

Goodridge, who was born in Vaughan, Ontario in 1852, followed his brother Henry to Edmonton in 1880. Soon after his arrival he operated a boarding house at 99 Street and Jasper Avenue, then opened the hotel the following year in 1882.

Goodridge and his wife had four children. An active worker in the community, he played a large role in establishing School District #7. Goodridge was involved in the founding of the police and fire departments and was elected to the first town council in 1892.

The Jasper House Hotel in 1890

NORTH-WEST MOUNTED POLICE STATION AND GUARDHOUSE

Station. From January to March 1886, the NWMP two-man patrol in Edmonton was based in a building located at approximately Namayo Avenue (97 Street) and Jasper Avenue.

Guard House. The guard house was located inside Fort Edmonton, and was rented from the Hudson's Bay Company. Inside were ten cells and a room for the duty guards.

When the NWMP "A" Division arrived in Edmonton in 1874 under Inspector W. D. Jarvis, the twenty-two men in his command were actually quartered at Fort Saskatchewan. This decision created a certain amount of dissatisfaction. As a result, Edmontonians pressured the government to move the barracks to Edmonton. In 1885, Edmonton became the Divisional Headquarters with the detachment being stationed in Fort Edmonton. Seven months later, however, the force moved back to Fort Saskatchewan, complaining that the barracks at Fort Edmonton were heavily infested with bugs and lice. There was also a shortage of hay in the Edmonton area.

NWMP post at Fort Edmonton

THE KENNETH McDONALD HOUSE, constructed by the McDonald family in 1886, stood at 9173 Jasper Avenue until 1967, when it was moved to Fort Edmonton Park. There is a possibility that some of the logs from McDonald's first house (built in 1871) were used in this structure. It remained in the family until the 1940s.

The McDonald homestead

Kenneth McDonald was born in Stornaway, Scotland in 1828. After entering the Hudson's Bay Company's service in 1847, he was sent to Canada in 1850 and assigned to Fort Pitt. There, he met and married Emma Rowland. The couple enjoyed a long and happy marriage, and raised seven children: William, Caroline, Flora, Betsy, Eliza, Catherine, and Alex.

In 1860 McDonald and his brother-in-law, William Rowland, staked claims on land overlooking the river valley, and thus became the first Hudson's Bay Company men to live outside the fort. McDonald took a sincere interest in the tiny community of Edmonton. He was among the group of men who established Edmonton's first school and who guaranteed the salary of the first teacher in 1881. He was a devout Presbyterian and helped to bring the first Presbyterian minister, the Reverend A. B. Baird, to Edmonton in 1882.

After leaving the Hudson's Bay Company, McDonald engaged in mixed farming. The farm enabled the family to be largely self-sufficient.

DOMINION LAND OFFICE. The original location of the Dominion Land Office was on Victoria Avenue (100 Avenue) at Second Street (102 Street). The building on Fort Edmonton Park's 1885 Street is not the original office, but is another building of the same era built about 1890 in Fort Saskatchewan. It was purchased from the Great North-West Pioneer Village in 1968.

The Dominion Land Offices administered the Dominion Land Act under whose terms intending settlers could be granted land newly acquired from the Hudson's Bay Company for a ten dollar fee and the requirement to construct a dwelling and cultivate a specified number of acres. The purpose of this policy was to encourage settlement in the Canadian West.

The Dominion Land Office in Edmonton was involved in what was known as the Land Office stoal. There was always considerable rivalry between Edmonton on the north side of the North Saskatchewan River and South Edmonton (later called Strathcona) on the south side. The rivalry came to a head in 1892 when the inhabitants of South Edmonton tried to have the Dominion Land Office moved there from Edmonton, convincing the federal government that the land office would be more convenient for new settlers if it were on the south side of the river. Agent Thomas Anderson started to move the office to South Edmonton, but was stopped by Edmonton's citizens. There was a flurry of excitement, and the home guards, organized for the Riel Rebellion of 1885, were recalled. The North-West Mounted Police arrived to help calm the situation.

The Dominion Land Office on 1885 Street

Urgent telegrams were sent to Ottawa, with the result that Sir Wilfred Laurier cancelled the proposed move.

TRANSPORTATION IN PRE-RAILWAY DAYS

The Stage Coach. When the term *stage coach* is mentioned, people usually think of the heavy Concord coaches featured in many western

movies. While the vehicle which ran from Edmonton to Calgary in later years resembled these, the earliest form of coach on the Calgary-Edmonton run was

An early stage coach struggles through the mud

nothing more than an open freight wagon with a hood at the rear to protect the passengers from the weather. The stage coach in use at Fort Edmonton Park is a replica of the later style.

The stage coach service began on August 4, 1883. A trip began at 9:00 a.m. every Monday morning at the Jasper House hotel in Edmonton arriving in Calgary the following Friday. The same schedule applied to those travelling from Calgary to Edmonton. The one-way fare was twenty-five dollars. The arrival of the Calgary and Edmonton Railway in Strathcona on July 27, 1891 marked the end of the stage coach service and of an era.

A later type of coach at Fort Edmonton

54

Original Locations of some 1885 Street buildings.

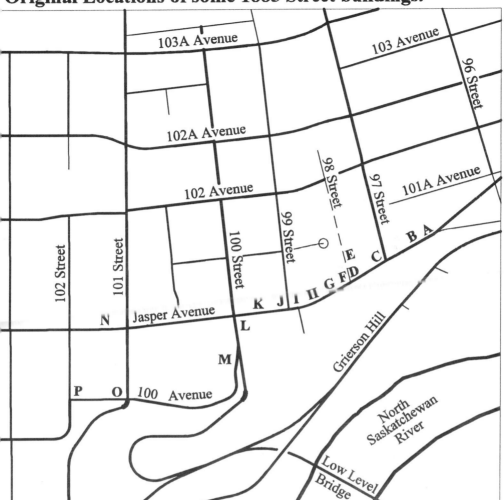

A NWMP Station	**J** McDonald's Carpenter Shop
B Jasper House Hotel	**K** Kernohan's Millinery Shop
C Sanderson and Looby's	Hutchings and Riley's
Blacksmith Shop	Harness
D Kelly's Saloon	**L** Bulletin Building
E Lauder's Bakery	**M** McCauley's Livery Stable
F McDougall's General Store	**N** Secord Fur Store
G Ross Brothers' Hardware	**O** McDougall Church
H Brynes' Shoe Shop	**P** Dominion Land Office
I Raymer's Jeweller	**Q** Daly's Drug Store
	105 Street south of 99 Avenue

Looking southeast towards the river from the firehall

Packing horses for the trip to the Klondyke at Secord Furs in 1898

1905 STREET - MUNICIPAL ERA (1892-1914)

1905 Street represents Edmonton in its development after the first train of the Calgary & Edmonton Railway arrived in South Edmonton (Strathcona) in 1891. The building of the Edmonton, Yukon & Pacific Railway from South Edmonton connecting the C & E Railway to the north side of the river in 1902 and the construction through Edmonton of the Canadian Northern Railway in 1904, all contributed to Edmonton's development from a small community to a thriving urban centre.

In 1905, when Edmonton became the capital of the newly-established province of Alberta, the city boasted a population of 14,000. In its earliest days, Edmonton's population had been largely British or French in origin, but with the coming of the railways, settlers poured into the province from Germany, Scandinavia, and Eastern Europe, dramatically changing the city's ethnic composition. In 1906 alone the population increased by 30 per cent.

While Edmonton had been incorporated as a town in 1892, it achieved city status in 1904 and began to take on the characteristics usually associated with modern urban life. Edmontonians had enjoyed electricity as early as 1891 and telephone service

North side of Jasper Avenue in 1904 looking east

since the 1880s. By 1908 Edmonton had its first streetcar and the first automatic dialing telephone service in North America. The year 1908 also saw the establishment of the University of Alberta in Strathcona, the municipality on the south bank of the North Saskatchewan River.

Industrial development centred on coal. Along the North Saskatchewan River, shallow shafts were sunk into its banks in search of the mineral. On the booming real estate front, speculators were frantically building paper fortunes. Even the Hudson's Bay Company was selling off its land reserves.

The buildings located on 1905 Street reflect this period, a time when businesses of all kinds were thriving, and people could afford to purchase more than just the bare necessities required for daily living.

South side of Jasper Avenue looking east

1905 Street

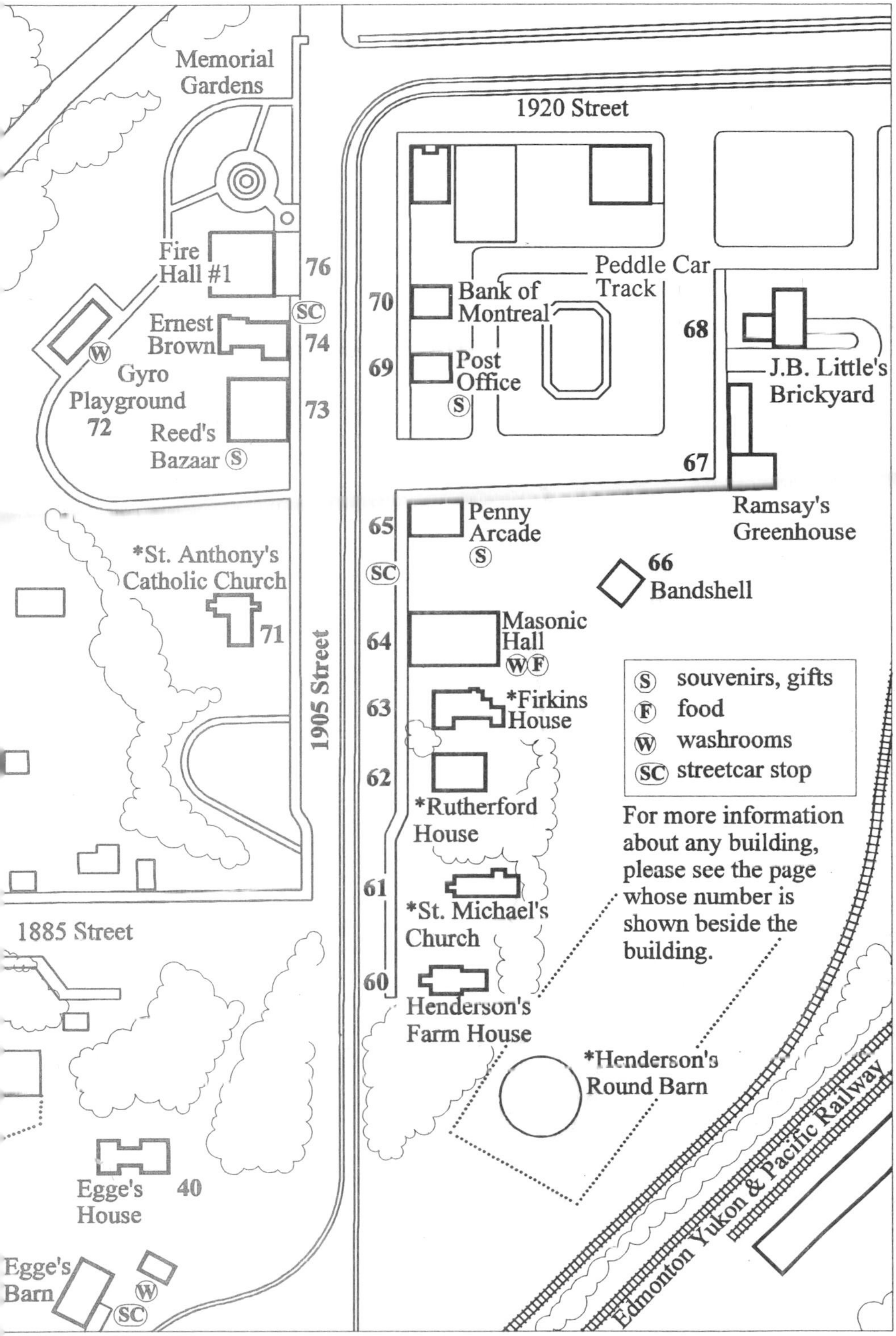

Memorial Gardens

1920 Street

Fire Hall #1

76

SC 74

Ernest Brown

W

Gyro Playground

72

73

Reed's Bazaar S

70 Bank of Montreal

Peddle Car Track

69 Post Office

S

68

J.B. Little's Brickyard

67

Ramsay's Greenhouse

*St. Anthony's Catholic Church

71

65 Penny Arcade S

SC

66 Bandshell

1905 Street

64 Masonic Hall W F

63 *Firkins House

62

*Rutherford House

61 *St. Michael's Church

60

Henderson's Farm House

1885 Street

S   souvenirs, gifts
F   food
W   washrooms
SC streetcar stop

For more information about any building, please see the page whose number is shown beside the building.

*Henderson's Round Barn

Edmonton Yukon & Pacific Railway

Egge's House   40

Egge's Barn

W

SC

* Original Buildings

THE HENDERSON HOMESTEAD. The Henderson homestead was located about one mile west of Whitemud Creek on Twenty-third Avenue in the Rabbit Hill area. While the house is a replica, the barn is the original round barn which Henderson built in 1898 after see-

ing similar structures in Ontario and Florida. It is one of the few surviving round barns in Canada.

The Henderson Family

Thomas Henderson was born in 1846 at North Oxford, Ontario. His wife, Margaret Oliver, was born in 1840 at Scarborough, Ontario. The couple were married in 1866 and lived for seven years in Ontario before moving to a small farm near Maple Ridge, British Columbia, where they resided for seven more years. The Hendersons had seven children.

In 1880, the family set out for Fort Edmonton after Henderson heard reports of gold being found in the river there. Before finally settling on their homestead at Rabbit Hill in 1891, the family farmed on several homesteads in the Edmonton area. In addition, Henderson worked as a carpenter and mined gold and coal with James Haney on the North Saskatchewan River near Rabbit Hill.

The Round Barn

He introduced the first swarm of honey bees to Edmonton and owned the first herd of Jersey cattle. Henderson was the moving force in the establishment of the Rabbit Hill School District in 1895 serving with B. Lendrum and G. MacDonald on its first school board.

ST. MICHAEL AND ALL ANGELS ANGLICAN CHURCH had its beginning in October 1909 when a small group in North Edmonton met one evening for a service conducted by the Reverend H. H. Summers of St. Paul's Anglican Church. Services continued to be held on Monday nights at Graham's lumber store, Reverend Summers having responsibilities in his own church on Sundays.

By 1910, services were held on Sunday mornings and had become the responsibility of a missionary, Walter Leversedge. Early that same year, members of the congregation decided to establish a separate parish to be known as St. Michael and All Angels. The new parish obtained land on the southeast corner of 127 Avenue and 69 Street, and construction of a church began.

St. Michael and All Angels Church

The next step was to request their own priest. On October 21, 1910, Reverend C. H. Bailey was placed in charge, being responsible as well for the mission church in the Calder district. At 7:00 p.m., November 20, 1910, Reverend Bailey held the first service in the new church even though its walls had not as yet been either plastered or painted. The church was consecrated by Bishop W. Cyprian Pinkham of Calgary, on December 1, 1910.

The little church continued to be used until the early 1970s. In 1972, the city informed the congregation that it planned to develop 127 Avenue, and would need the property on which the church was situated for the project. Rather than see their beloved church demolished, the congregation tried to find it a new home. In May, 1974 the parish obtained a government grant to cover the cost of moving the structure to Fort Edmonton Park. The church underwent a major rebuilding at the Park and, on June 28, 1988, was reconsecrated by Bishop Kenneth Genge of the Edmonton diocese.

THE RUTHERFORD HOUSE was the home from 1895 to 1911 of Alberta's first premier. In 1911 the family moved to the brick house which still stands on the University of Alberta campus.

Premier Rutherford's first house, a one–story frame structure, was located in Strathcona at Fifth Avenue N. E. and Main Street (8715 104 Street). A second story, including a central staircase and four bedrooms, was added in 1899 as were the veranda and the brick fireplace in the study. During the next five years, a three-room addition was built above the kitchen and the former porch.

Alexander Cameron Rutherford was born in Ontario in 1857. He received a bachelor of civil law degree from McGill University and practiced law in Kemptville, Ontario. In 1895 he moved with his wife Mattie and their two children to South Edmonton (Strathcona) where he was admitted to the North West Territories bar.

When South Edmonton became the town of Strathcona in 1899, Rutherford became its first secretary-treasurer. In 1902 he was elected Strathcona's representative to the legislative assembly and shortly afterward became deputy speaker of the House. In August 1905 he was elected president of the Alberta Liberal Association, and when Alberta became a province that September, he was asked by Lieutenant-Governor George Bulyea to form the province's first government.

One of Premier Rutherford's first projects was the establishment of the University of Alberta in 1908. Rutherford was also responsible for the selection of the site of the Alberta legislature buildings.

The Rutherfords at their house in Strathcona

THE FIRKINS HOUSE, built in 1912 by a dentist, Dr. Ashley Firkins, and his wife Blanche, originally stood at 7821 Saskatchewan Drive. The house represents the open-plan concept which began to have an impact on residential architecture prior to the First World War. Before this, each room in a house tended to be closed off from the others. In the open-plan house, the living room, dining room, and front entrance flow into each other, their boundaries marked by arches and built-in furniture which permit a more effective use of space. The Firkins house is a modern semi-bungalow, a

The Firkins house just before it was moved

style popular throughout the 1920s as a middle class home. It is also an example of the craftsman influence which favoured a more natural choice of materials in construction. Highly ornate exteriors, which typified its predecessors, have been replaced by straight, uncluttered lines.

The Firkins family occupied the house until 1923 when it was purchased by Robert Newton, a university professor. A year later, Newton sold the house to an entomology professor, Colonel E. H. Strickland, who lived there until his retirement in 1954. At this time, professor Douglas Crosby and his wife Janet purchased the home. They later sold the house to Rod and Audrey Karpetz who donated it to Fort Edmonton Park in 1992.

Unlike others of its era still in existence in the Edmonton area, the Firkins house has seen very little in the way of major alterations. As a result, it remains a faithful example of its type.

63

THE MASONIC HALL. The earliest reference to the Masonic Lodge in Edmonton can be found in the December 3, 1881 issue of *The Bulletin*. The article mentions a meeting of local Masons held in McDougall Hall to organize the first lodge in the community, to be known as Saskatchewan Lodge #17. Unfortunately, the lodge had some difficulty in maintaining itself and surrendered its charter in 1889. However, with the improvement in Edmonton's economic climate after the coming of the railway in 1892, a new lodge (Lodge #52) was organized. As the number of Masons increased, it became necessary in 1901 to form yet another lodge, Jasper Lodge #78.

The Masonic Hall, built in 1903 by the Masonic Order, stood at Victoria Avenue and Second Street (10044-48 102 Street). Alberta College rented the main floor from 1903 to 1905. In 1905 the Edmonton offices of the Dominion government's Customs and Inland Revenue Departments moved in. An addition was built in March, 1906, and the Edmonton Cigar Factory joined the government offices. The Inland Revenue office was relocated in 1908, and the Customs House the following year. For a short time, an electrical contracting firm, the Electric Construction Company, rented space as did McManus Brothers Real Estate.

The Masons occupied the upper floor until they moved in 1931 to their new temple on 100 Avenue. The old hall was then sold to the

Edmonton Tent and Awning Company and torn down in 1951.

The replica of the Masonic Hall includes a Masonic museum on its second floor with visitor food services on the street level.

The Masonic Hall in the 1940s

THE PENNY ARCADE BUILDING was located on First Street at Elizabeth Street (101 Street at 102 Avenue), the site of the present Eaton Centre. In the early 1900s it was common for enterprises such as shooting galleries or pool halls to share a building with other offices. In the case of the Penny Arcade, the space was shared with an employment office and cartage company, a convenient combination for the young man seeking employment but with time on his hands.

The Penny Arcade building, at the right, on 101 Street next to the King Edward Hotel

The International Employment Agency was located in the Penny Arcade building from 1912 to 1914. The agency was operated by Andrew J. Adams who also ran the Adams Express and Cartage Company until 1913. The combination of an express and employment office was also common. One reason for this combination was that those who ran cartage companies could readily hire labourers and teamsters from the pool of unemployed men passing through the employment office.

Shooting galleries originated in France and England as private target practice facilities for those planning to engage in pistol duels. In Edmonton, such places were considered low-class establishments where drifters, trouble makers, and the unemployed spent their time. In addition to shooting galleries, penny arcades often included such other attractions as peep shows, grip testing devices, strength testers, and fortune telling machines. The fortune telling machine in the Penny Arcade on 1905 Street is a palm-reading type. Women usually did not frequent penny arcades.

THE EAST END PARK BANDSHELLwas built about 1913 in Borden Park, then known as East End Park. Band concerts in the park were a popular summer pastime with Edmontonians. Concerts might be held as early as April and continue on into October, depending on the weather. In 1912, band concerts were held in the park on Wednesdays, Saturdays, and Sundays. Often as many as 3,000 people attended these concerts, and extra streetcar service had to be provided to accommodate the crowds.

Before the First World War, between 1911 and 1914, Edmonton had six major bands which played in bandshells throughout the city. This form of entertainment was so popular with the public, that the bands were awarded financial grants by the city so that they could continue to perform. Bands which played in the East End Park included the Citizens' Band, the 101st Regiment Band, the Moose Band, and the Salvation Army Band. A typical concert included several marches, waltzes, solos, and overtures.

A concert at the East End Park Bandshell

RAMSAY'S GREENHOUSES were located at 100 Avenue and 111 Street. Five were built in 1906 with four more added following the success of the first five. Ramsay's were the first greenhouses in northern Alberta, and their Good Friday open houses, started in 1906, were a popular event with winter-weary Edmontonians. Ramsay's favorite flowers were roses and carnations to which he devoted five of the greenhouses. The other

Ramsay's Greenhouses

four were used for potting bulbs and raising bedding plants, along with a wide assortment of flowers and tropical plants which were the favorites of the time. Imported bulbs and seeds from the Netherlands and Belgium were the mainstays of his business.

Business went well for Ramsay despite the First World War and the collapse of his first five greenhouses in 1935 during a heavy snowfall. However, the Second World War interrupted his supply of bulbs from the Lowlands, and he eventually abandoned the wholesale business to concentrate on his retail trade. The firm continued in business until 1983 but at a different address.

Walter Ramsay was born in Ontario on August 19, 1870. He became a teacher, and in 1897 decided to move west. He taught for one year at Clover Bar, then became first assistant at the public school in Edmonton. In 1903 he was appointed principal of the new Queens Avenue Public School.

In 1901 Ramsay married Lucy McRae. The couple, who later raised two children, purchased a home on Elizabeth Street near Howard (102 Avenue and 100A Street). His first greenhouse was built in its backyard. He began seriously to consider going into the florist trade, and in December 1905, submitted his resignation to the school board in order to raise flowers on a full-time basis.

J. B. LITTLE'S BRICKYARD includes the firm's original brick-making machinery housed in a replica building. James B. Little, a native of Scotland, arrived in Edmonton in 1892. Prior to this, Little made bricks for the construction of the Banff Springs Hotel, and was a partner in the Calgary brickmaking firm of Little & Maloney. In Edmonton, Little purchased ten acres in the Riverdale community for the purpose of establishing another brickyard. The site contained large deposits of river-terrace clay suitable for brickmaking. Little employed the soft-mud mold process to make his bricks. The large, deep clay pits, since filled in, were a familiar part of Riverdale.

The building boom resulting from the arrival of the railway in 1891 meant that brickyards in the area did not lack for business. By July 1893, Little & Maloney fired its first Edmonton kiln. Some time later, Little became the sole owner of this operation which became known as Little's Brickyard. He expanded his business by buying out his two nearby competitors.

Little and his family maintained close ties with the Riverdale community, employing its teenagers to hand-turn drying bricks, and sponsoring its community baseball and hockey teams. He donated the land for the new Riverdale school as well as the bricks for its construction. His sons David and John worked closely with their father and took over operation of the company at his death in 1939.

In 1958 the brickyard closed. There was no more clay, and the skilled operators required for the brick making machinery had become increasingly hard to find.

The machinery in operation at Little's brickyard

THE POST OFFICE BLOCK, built about 1893 by Edmiston and Wilson, was located at what is now 9823 Jasper Avenue. The replica of this building on 1905 Street houses three businesses: the post office, the telephone exchange, and H. C. Taylor's law office. The equipment on the roof is typical of early telephone exchanges. Edmonton had enjoyed telephone service to St. Albert as early as January 1885, thanks to the efforts of Alex Taylor.

In July 1893, after much controversy over the choice of location, the post office was established on the main floor of this building. The central telephone exchange office moved in on the second floor on November 1, 1894. H. C. Taylor had his law office across the hall from the telephone exchange from January to December 1896.

In December 1898, the telephone exchange moved down the street to the third floor of the Gariepy Block. On May 9, 1906, the post office was also relocated to McDougall and Rice

The Edmiston and Post Office Blocks

Streets (100 Street and 101A Avenue), after which the floor space was renovated for the Mariaggi Cafe.

Through the years the building housed many different businesses. Parts of it were used as a furniture store, a furrier, a barber shop, and a photography studio. Its offices were rented by insurance agencies, a watchmaker, and even a filing and grinding company. In 1899 the Edmiston Block was constructed adjoining the Post Office Block, and access to the second floor of the new structure was gained through the stairway in the Post Office Block.

The building was torn down in 1961, and the site used as a parking lot until 1981 when it became part of Edmonton's Convention Centre.

THE BANK OF MONTREAL, located on the north side of Jasper Avenue between Queens Avenue (99 Street) and Fraser Avenue (98 Street), was owned by Phillip Heiminck. Heiminck, a realtor, occupied the building from the mid 1890s until September 1903, when he sold it to the Bank of Montreal. The bank occupied the structure until February 1905 when it moved into its new building at the corner of Howard Street (100A Street) and Jasper Avenue.

The Heiminck Building (centre) in 1902

The Bank of Montreal, whose first manager was Edwin Charles Pardee, was the sixth bank to be established in Edmonton. The honour of being the first bank in the city goes to the Imperial Bank of Canada (now the Canadian Imperial Bank of Commerce) who opened its first branch in September 1892.

Prior to 1903, the second floor of Heiminck's building was rented to Frank Deggendorpher, a local architect. After the Bank of Montreal departed, the next tenant was the real estate firm of Brunton and Hitchings who remained until 1907. From 1907 until 1925 the building was occupied by three different clothiers. Vacant from 1925 to 1929, the building's last tenant was the Davies Furniture Exchange who occupied the building until the early 1930s. In 1934 it was demolished.

ST. ANTHONY'S CHURCH AND SCHOOL was built in 1894 as the Church of St. Anthony of Padua. The tiny chapel was located south of the river at First Street S.W. and Second Avenue N.W. (105 Street and 84 Avenue). From the early 1880s to 1905, the Catholic community in Strathcona was served by the Oblate Fathers from St. Joachim's parish on the north side of the river. In 1905, Father F. G. Nordmann took up residence within St. Anthony's parish.

In November 1894, St. Anthony's Separate School District Number 12 of the Northwest Territories was founded, and classes were held in the little church. The district advertised for a teacher in February 1895, but owing to the difficulty of keeping one, two nuns from the order of the Faithful Companions of Jesus, Mother Hannah O'Neill and Mother Julia Theresa Coglan took over the teaching. To give some idea of their commitment, the sisters lived on the north side of the river at 99 Avenue and 110 Street, and commuted daily to the school, probably crossing the river by means of John Walter's ferry. In 1902 the sisters were replaced by lay teachers.

By 1897 the church was already overcrowded and funds were raised for a new and larger structure which was completed in 1903. In 1901, the school addition was added to the original building and

was used until 1906 when a larger school was constructed. Both the old wooden school and chapel and the newer brick church were purchased in 1946 by the Ukrainian Catholic rite who took possession in 1949

St. Anthony's Church and School on 84 Avenue

when the new St. Anthony's Church was opened on 82 Avenue at 106 Street. The brick church, re-named St. Basil's by the Ukrainian parishioners, was used until 1968 when a larger St. Basil's was constructed at 7007 109 Street.

St. Anthony's Church - Knights of Columbus - Southgate Developments Ltd.

GYRO PARK. The playground movement in North America evolved after the turn of the century in the belief that there was a need for such facilities for citizens living in the inner cities. Since recruitment in the First World War showed that many Canadians were physically unfit for service, various organizations established playgrounds to change this. Gyro Clubs and other service groups increasingly focused on children's activities, providing playgrounds in an effort to help improve the health of future generations.

On August 19, 1922, the first Gyro playground was opened at Patricia Square (now Giovanni Caboto Park located at 95 Street

and 108 Avenue). To raise money for playground equipment, the club began the popular Gyro carnival which was held for many years. A parade along Jasper Avenue opened the week-long carnival which included bands,

Children at an early Gyro Park

dancers, tumblers, and clowns. Eight more Gyro Parks were built over the years, the last in 1949. Each year the parks opened for the summer season on May 24.

Beginning about 1925 the city of Edmonton and the Gyro Club began to share the operation and maintenance of the parks, but in 1944 full responsibility was taken over by the city's newly-formed Parks and Recreation Department.

REED'S BAZAAR (THE LEE BLOCK), built by Robert Lee in 1905, stood on Jasper Avenue at Second Street (102 Street). There were two spacious rooms on the ground floor and ten rooms or offices on the second floor. The first tenant on the main floor was W. A. Cameron, a well-known painter and wall paper hanger who also sold furniture. Other tenants included a Mr. Martin. On the second floor were two architects: Percy R. Barnes and J. D. Johnson; two physicians: Dr. A. R. Cunningham and Dr. W. O. Farquharson, and a tailor, W. Morritt.

When Cameron moved out of the Lee Block, his premises were taken over by William Reed, who came to Edmonton from Ontario in 1905. Reed opened a tea room and store on the main floor. The new business opened on November 25, 1905 and rapidly became very popular.

At first Reed took the whole main floor, but on February 1, 1906, the real estate firm owned by W. S. Weeks and A. W. Taylor rented the west side of the main floor from Reed. The most likely reason for Reed's action was that the main floor space was too large for his needs. Reed hired the original architect, J. H. Millar, to divide the main floor into two large stores.

The real estate firm rented the west side for only a year and a half. They were succeeded first by the Oriental Trading Company, then a year later by Manasse and Eaton Ladies' Wear, and finally by Sage Appleton & Company, another real estate firm.

Reed's Bazaar

continued on next page

REED'S BAZAAR (continued)

In 1912, an Edmonton businessman, George Brown, signed a ninety-nine year lease with Lee. Brown proposed to build a ten-story office building on the corner where the Lee Block stood, the first high rise in Edmonton. The complex, which was never constructed, was to include the Pantages Theatre. To carry out Brown's plans, the Lee Block had to be removed. On the night of January 11, 1913, however, the Lee Block was totally destroyed in a fire. Reed's losses would have been greater except that he had already begun to move his stock, which was covered by insurance, into new premises at 9948 Jasper Avenue.

THE ERNEST BROWN PHOTOGRAPHIC STUDIO was located on the north side of Jasper Avenue between 96 and 97 Streets, on the site of the present Brighton Block. The building was originally constructed in 1897 by the photographer C. W. Mathers and was used as his studio and residence until 1900. In about 1903 Mathers extended the front top portion of the building. Brown purchased the structure in 1904 and in 1907 had plate glass windows installed across the entire front. At the same time he renovated the front office. In 1911 he began construction next door of the first part of the three-story Brown Block. To make room for the new structure, the old studio was moved from the property in 1912.

Ernest Brown was born September 8, 1877 in Middlesborough, Yorkshire, England. He was apprenticed at an early age to the photographer James Bacon of Newcastle-on-Tyne. Brown married Molly Carr in 1902. In the fall of the same year, since times were hard in England, Brown set out alone for Toronto where he worked at a variety of odd jobs. Later, when Brown was hired by Mathers as the manager for his studio in Edmonton, he returned to England for Molly, and the couple arrived in Edmonton on April 18, 1904. They had two children, one of whom died in infancy.

Brown managed Mathers' studio for a few months, then made a deal to purchase the portrait part of the business on August 1, 1904. Later he also purchased Mathers' extensive view collection,
continued on next page

THE ERNEST BROWN STUDIO (continued)

a decision which in time would prove to be both historically and financially profitable. Business was good until 1915 when the war took its toll. Brown managed to weather the hard times until the early 1920s when a loan company foreclosed on his property. For a time Brown lost his enthusiasm for business.

In 1926, a young man in Vegreville persuaded Brown to show him how to operate his newly-acquired studio, an operation which Brown eventually took over. In 1933 Brown moved back to Edmonton and from that time until the war began, set up and successfully managed a display of his historical photographs and other material. His exhibit, *The Birth of the West*, displayed in Haddon Hall, was the first museum in Edmonton. The collection is now housed in the provincial archives. This guidebook contains many of Ernest Brown's photographs.

Mathers' original photographic studio

FIRE HALL #1 was built on Fraser Avenue north of Jasper Avenue (10126 98 Street). The town had been incorporated in 1892, and the first meetings of the town council were held in various public halls. The fire hall also moved about from place to place. When the town took possession of the new building on Fraser Avenue on December 20, 1893, Fire Hall #1, the police station, the town offices, and the council chambers, all moved into the new structure.

The building remained more or less unaltered for some years, although a room was provided in 1897 for the Board of Trade. Slight changes were also made in the firemen's quarters.

Fire Hall #1 in 1908

Between 1900 and 1905, the building became increasingly inadequate owing to the town's rapid expansion. The fact that the old building was settling and was considered to be unsafe persuaded the 1904 council to consider plans for a new city offices building. The new structure, called the Civic Annex, was intended to house only the civic offices and the police department. It was built next door to the fire hall which would now be used solely by the firemen. The building was occupied in late December, 1904.

The old fire hall was not significantly altered, although interior plumbing was installed in 1905, a new stable was built, and a new hose and bell tower were added. Few major alterations were made until 1930 when the fire department left. After 1930 it housed different associations until it was demolished in 1958.

HORSES AND HORSELESS CARRIAGES. When J. H. Morris returned from Winnipeg on May 25, 1904 with the first automobile to be seen in Edmonton, the event marked the beginning of a new era of transportation in the province's capital. The car, a two cylinder model, also had the distinction of being the first car in the city to run out of gas, a misfortune which took place the following evening while Morris and some of his friends were out for a trial run. Early automobile owners were nothing if not resourceful, and Morris borrowed a tin of

The opening of the provincial legislature

benzine, a form of petroleum used as a cleaner, from a neighboring farm house enabling the car to return to the city on one cylinder.

Until this historic moment, and, indeed for many years after, the horse played an important role in transportation in Edmonton. When Lieutenant Governor Bulyea rode to the opening of the first provincial legislature, it was in the carriage shown in the accompanying photograph, the same carriage which is now in Fort Edmonton Park's collection. The visitor to the Park will find other horse-drawn vehicles there - Lauder's bakery delivery wagon, the two street sprinklers, buggies, sleighs, an ox cart, and even a prairie schooner.

The city's thriving construction industry is represented by horse-pulled scoops and a hopper wagon for carrying away earth from excavations. Many examples of earlier, specialized farming equipment are also to be found throughout the Park.

77

EDMONTON, YUKON, AND PACIFIC RAILWAY. The locomotive and passenger coaches which operate at Fort Edmonton Park are lettered to honour the railway which in 1902 became the first to connect the towns of Edmonton and Strathcona. The EY&P's line began at 63 Avenue and 103 Street, and at its greatest length in 1906, ran along the north bank of the North Saskatchewan River, finally reaching Stony Plain Road and 123 Street. A ceremony held April 29, 1954, marked the end of full operation over its entire length, although parts of the line remained in operation until the early 1970s. The last section was used to carry freight cars to Gainers' packing plant at Mill Creek on Edmonton's south side.

The name Edmonton, Yukon, and Pacific resulted from the ambitions of Edmonton's town council who obtained a charter for the line in 1896. The charter mentioned routes to the Pacific Ocean by way of the Yellowhead Pass and to the Yukon by way of the Athabasca and Peace Rivers. The main objective of council, however, was to get a railway across the North Saskatchewan River. Edmonton's development was being held back for lack of such a connection, since freight from the east had to be hauled into the town from the end of the railway on the south side of the river by wagon, cart, or sleigh (all of which proved inefficient for large quantities) or shipped by river boat.

If Edmonton were to become a great metropolis, it would need a rail link. For a time, Edmonton's citizens believed that the answer to their problems lay in the Calgary and Edmonton Railroad Company (C&E) whose first train arrived in South Edmonton (Strathcona) on August 10, 1891. It soon became clear, however, that the C & E (operated by the Canadian Pacific Railway) had no intention of crossing the river, possibly because of the cost of bridge construction. Edmontonians could only look on in frustration while the hamlet of Strathcona, now the head of rail, boomed. The Canadian Pacific Railway eventually crossed the North Saskatchewan River, but not until the High Level Bridge was opened in 1913.

Since the Canadian Pacific Railway did not appear to be interested in crossing the river, the Edmonton District Railway Company was formed by members of Edmonton's town council. The new company

continued on next page

was sold in 1898 to the railway developers William MacKenzie and Donald Mann who promptly re-named the as yet unbuilt railway, the Edmonton, Yukon, and Pacific Railway (EY&P). The new railway received a major boost when the Federal Government built the Low Level Bridge in 1900, thereby providing a means for the line of crossing the river. In 1901 construction began on the first 7.2 kilometre (4.5 mile) section which ran through Mill Creek Ravine, across the Low Level Bridge, and ended at Donald Ross's hotel located at the foot of McDougall Hill just below the present MacDonald Hotel. The first train, pulled by Canadian Northern Railway's #26, including a passenger coach, a box car, and two flat cars, arrived at the McDougall Hill station on October 20, 1902 at 4:00 p.m. (The Canadian Northern Railway was also owned by MacKenzie and Mann).

In 1904, the EY&P was extended west 5.1 kilometres (3.2 miles) to 123 Street following a winding route (parts of which are still visible) above the Victoria Golf Course and down Wadhurst Road. The first train over this extension ran on June 16, 1907. Along with its parent company, the Canadian Northern Railway, the Edmonton, Yukon, and Pacific Railway became part of the Canadian National Railways.

While the EY&P only enjoyed a few years of real importance between 1902 and 1904, it represented the first stage in making Edmonton a major railway centre.

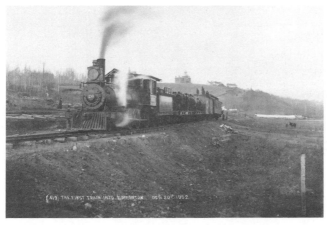

The first EY&P train arrives in Edmonton, October 20, 1902

THE STEAM TRAIN AT FORT EDMONTON PARK is lettered to honour Edmonton's first railway, the Edmonton, Yukon & Pacific. The locomotive and cars come from as far apart as Louisiana and Northern Alberta.

Locomotive 107 is a prairie type (2-6-2) locomotive built by the Baldwin Locomotive Works at Philadelphia, Pennsylvania (builder's number 52255) in September 1919. Its classification as a 2-6-2 means that there are two leading, or pony wheels, six driving wheels, and two trailing wheels. For fifty years it operated in Louisiana.

The open coach, #210, was converted to its present appearance from a former Northern Alberta Railways (NAR) caboose donated to the Park by the NAR's successor, the Canadian National Railways. The two larger coaches, #300 and #304, were built about 1905 by the Canadian Pacific Railway. The coaches operated for many years on the NAR and recall the days when the CPR was responsible for the NAR's management. The coaches were acquired by the Fort Edmonton Historical Foundation and substantially rebuilt. The Foundation also owns former NAR business car *Peace River* which is in storage at Fort Edmonton Park. The railway line in the Park is four kilometres (2.5 miles) long.

The train at Fort Edmonton Park

THE EDMONTON RADIAL RAILWAY, the city's street railway system, is the direct ancestor both of Edmonton Transit, which today provides bus and light rail transit service in the city, and of the Edmonton Radial Railway Society, which provides streetcar service in Fort Edmonton Park. (The term *radial* implies that the lines of the street railway radiate out from the city centre.)

Streetcar service in Edmonton began in 1908. A short trial run was made on October 29, 1908, and the first informal operation took place the following evening. Scheduled service did not begin until November 9, and then only in Edmonton itself. At that time, the only road access to the city of Strathcona was by means of the Low Level Bridge which had to be shared with the trains of the Edmonton, Yukon, and Pacific Railway, as well as with vehicular and horse-drawn traffic. The first streetcar ran to Strathcona over the Low Level Bridge on December 4, 1908.

After 1908, a number of extensions were added to the street railway, including the spectacular route over the Canadian Pacific Railway's High Level Bridge. The new bridge, completed in 1913, was a double deck structure with a roadway on the lower level and three tracks on the upper deck. CPR trains ran on the middle track, and the street railway operated on the outer two. With the inauguration of streetcar service

Streetcars on Jasper Avenue in 1911

over the imposing structure on August 11, 1913, the long trip to Strathcona from Edmonton was considerably shortened.

For many years no new equipment was purchased by the street railway. Then in 1930, five new, steel-bodied cars, the most up-to-date equipment then available, were placed in service. Equipped with

81

leather seats, they were immediately popular with the passengers. One of the series, #80, has been located and restored by members of the Edmonton Radial Railway Society for operation in the Park.

Based on trial operations of a demonstrator bus loaned to the street railway in 1930, the Edmonton Radial Railway purchased a total of four gas buses, including the demonstrator. The new equipment was used both to replace existing streetcar lines and to open new routes such as the line to the University of Alberta. Trolley buses were introduced to the city in 1939 when the old streetcar route from Whyte Avenue, across the Low Level Bridge, and up the hill past the legislature buildings, was converted to electric bus operation.

During the Second World War the system's cars and trackage suffered heavy wear, and if the streetcars were to be kept, much of the system would have to be rebuilt. In addition, the city's growth after the war produced new subdivisions not accessible by the then existing streetcar lines. The decision was made to abandon the faithful cars and to replace them with gas or trolley buses.

Five types of transportation in Edmonton

When streetcar #52 rolled into Cromdale carbarn in the early hours of September 2, 1951, most Edmontonians firmly believed that they had seen the last of streetcar operation in Alberta's capital city. The faithful cars were sold to become tool sheds, summer cottages, restaurants, and one unfortunate, a pig pen. Fortunately, members of the Edmonton Radial Railway Society have managed to acquire and restore several of Edmonton's former streetcars which they now operate in the Park.

1920 STREET - METROPOLITAN ERA (1914 - 1929)

The buildings and industries located on 1920 Street each represent some aspect of life in Edmonton in the period from 1919 to 1929. While Edmonton experienced an economic depression from about 1920 to 1923, the period which followed was one of prosperity, at least until the great stock market crash of 1929. The years of prosperity saw the growth of many small businesses whose beginnings are represented on 1885 and 1905 Streets, a number of which grew to become wholesalers and distributors. Construction boomed, and the bricks from J.B. Little's Brickyard were used throughout the city in the construction of factories, warehouses, schools, churches, and homes.

At the Mellon farm, the gas-powered tractors represent the transition from horse to tractor in the field of agriculture, while the farm itself typifies the small family-owned farms which had grown steadily in numbers across the prairies. The large warehouses of Edmonton's businesses of the 1920s played a major role in supplying these farms with their requirements.

Jasper Avenue looking west in 1920

As early as 1891, groups of immigrants - German, Ukrainian and others - settled many of the farms around Edmonton as did French and English settlers from eastern Canada. While immigration declined immediately after the First World War, the descendants of earlier immigrants, as well as many other newcomers to Canada in the post-war period, settled in the cities, including Edmonton. The influence of at least two groups of immigrants is reflected in the Ukrainian Bookstore and in the Al Raschid Mosque. Each institution served as a unifying centre for the people whose language, culture, and religion are represented there.

Other buildings reflect changes in daily living in the city itself. Bill's Confectionery with its soda bar had its counterpart in every city and town across North America. While restaurants and cafés had been common for many years, the soda bar represented a more casual form of entertainment. Another new form of entertainment was the automobile. For those fortunate enough to be able to afford one, the automobile provided a means of extending family outings. Just as the blacksmith and harness shops on 1885 Street looked after the needs of the horse, so the Motordrome on 1920 Street looked after those of the automobile - gas, oil, tires, and, all too often in those days, repairs.

For Edmontonians whose incomes did not permit automobile ownership, the streetcars housed in the Strathcona carbarn and its northside counterpart, Cromdale, provided a means of transportation to their place of employment, to Edmonton's downtown stores, and to the city's parks and other attractions.

In 1927, Edmontonians witnessed the opening of Blatchford Field, the forerunner of the present Municipal Airport. With its opening, Edmonton was able to expand the role of the little fur trading fort on the North Saskatchewan, but on a much vaster scale, as aircraft departed from the new airport for all parts of the North.

1920 Street

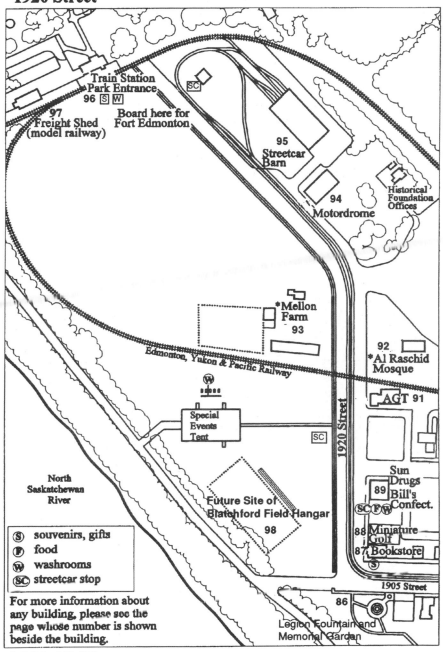

Train Station
Park Entrance
96 Ⓢ Ⓦ

97
Freight Shed
(model railway)

Board here for
Fort Edmonton

SC

95
Streetcar
Barn

94
Motordrome

Historical
Foundation
Offices

*Mellon
Farm
93

92
*Al Raschid
Mosque

Edmonton, Yukon & Pacific Railway

Ⓦ

Special
Events
Tent

SC

AGT 91

1920 Street

North
Saskatchewan
River

Future Site of
Blatchford Field Hangar
98

Sun
Drugs
89 Bill's
Confect.
SC Ⓕ Ⓦ

88 Miniature
Golf

87 Bookstore
Ⓢ

1905 Street

86
Legion Fountain and
Memorial Garden

Ⓢ souvenirs, gifts
Ⓕ food
Ⓦ washrooms
SC streetcar stop

For more information about
any building, please see the
page whose number is shown
beside the building.

* Original Buildings

LEGION FOUNTAIN AND MEMORIAL GARDEN. The Memorial Garden is representative of formal gardens typical of the Edwardian period and serves as a quiet rest spot for visitors to Fort Edmonton Park.

The garden's fountain, erected by the Royal Canadian Legion, serves as a monument to those who lost their lives in the First World War. The Legion, originally known as the Great War Veterans' Association, was formed to look after the interests of veterans of that conflict. The Association later changed its name to the Royal Canadian Legion.

The memorial garden and fountain at Fort Edmonton Park

THE UKRAINIAN BOOKSTORE (KOERMANN BLOCK) in Fort Edmonton Park is a replica of the building as it looked in 1919. The original Koermann Block is still located at 10232 - 96 Street. The building, opened in 1913, contained two stores in front, one rental space in the rear, and apartments on the second floor.

The Ukrainian Bookstore, known also as the *Ukrainska Knyharnia*, moved into one of the front stores in November 1914. It shared the main floor with Gustave Koermann who published the German language newspaper *Alberta Herold*. As the bookstore prospered and expanded, it eventually took over the entire front part of the main floor, while Koermann moved his printing business to the small space at the rear. In 1925 the bookstore moved to new quarters on 101 Street, and in 1965, to its present location at 10215 - 97 Street.

The Ukrainian Bookstore soon became well-known to Edmontonians, and to Ukrainians throughout Alberta, who, when travelling to Edmonton, made a point of visiting it. Here they could buy books and newspapers in their own language, obtain information about Ukrainian professional people such as doctors, dentists, lawyers, veterinarians, interpreters, translators, and others. At the store they could meet old friends or make new ones, hear the latest political and social news, discuss their problems, and obtain advice. Its customers could also purchase a variety of music and other goods from Ukraine. The Ukrainian Bookstore soon became the literary and cultural centre of the Ukrainian community.

The Ukrainian Bookstore on 96 Street in 1922

TOM THUMB MINIATURE GOLF COURSE. The original miniature golf courses provided serious golfers with a means of practicing their putting skills. In 1929 Garnet and Freida Carter, innkeepers in Tennessee, added a series of obstacles to their course and patented this approach under the name *Tom Thumb,* a name which recalls the tiny character from a children's story. Webb's Tom Thumb Golf Course, which is shown in the accompanying photograph, was built following the Carter's design. It was located at 8615 - 109 Street.

Miniature golf courses were soon established all over the continent, and Edmonton apparently shared the enthusiasm for the sport. The summer of 1930 saw no fewer than five miniature golf courses established in the area. Although the initial popularity of miniature golf peaked in the early 1930s, Edmonton is again witnessing a revival of interest in the game in the 1990s.

Webb's miniature golf course at night

THE SUN DRUGSTORE AND BILL'S CONFECTIONERY are replicas of the original businesses located at the corner of 109 Street and Jasper Avenue. In May 1922, the architectural firm of G. H. MacDonald and H. A. Magoon prepared a set of plans for a store building for Sidney Millward, a pharmacist. Initially the building consisted of a corner drugstore (the Sun) and two smaller stores. The Sun Drugstore was named after a Los Angeles business.

In 1930, Millward sold the drugstore to his brother Thomas who had worked there as a pharmacist since the early 1920s. In 1952 Thomas Millward sold the business to Edward C. Richards who had been a pharmacist at Sun Drugs since 1936. In 1956 the business was renamed Richard's Pharmacy and existed as such until 1963.

The space next to the drugstore was rented to Gordon King who ran a confectionery in it, the other premises being operated as a restaurant. Neither lasted very long, and about 1926 Millward combined the two smaller stores and rented them to William Thoucididuo (known as William Kazakos) and John Afaganis. The two Greek proprietors operated Bill's Confectionery. Bill's was known for its excellent confectionery including such customer favorites as turkish delight, chocolates, peanut butter puffs, and divinity fudge.

Bill's Confectionery was operated by Kazakos until 1947 when it was purchased by Bing Mah who operated it until 1955. The confectionery then became the Readi-Maid Bakery, a business which lasted only one year. Over the succeeding years a variety of firms occupied the two stores. By 1967 the building had been torn down to make way for the office tower known as the Executive Building which now stands on the same site.

Sidney Millward was born in 1894 in a suburb of Stratford-on-Avon. His older brother Alfred came to Edmonton in 1904 and worked as a locomotive engineer for the Canadian Northern Railway. Sidney and their mother followed in 1913. He became an apprentice in J. N. C. Hill's Drugstore and was later a member of the first graduating class of the Faculty of Pharmacy at the University of Alberta in 1916.

Kazakos was born in the Turkish town of Triglia. He was brought to Canada in 1910. At first he went to Winnipeg where he attended school. He then entered the confectionery business which his uncles operated at Portage Avenue and Main Street. Later, he was sent to Saskatoon where he managed a confectionery for his uncles before opening his own store in Edmonton with John Afaganis as his partner.

Sun Drugs and Bill's Confectionery in 1922

THE ALBERTA GOVERNMENT TELEPHONES' ST. PAUL EXCHANGE, built in 1929 at St. Paul, Alberta, is typical of numerous exchanges built across the province in the 1920s by

The AGT Telephone Exchange at the Park

Alberta Government Telephones (AGT). Their quaint, cottage-like exteriors, commonly of a clinker brick bungalow design, symbolized the *Silent Partner* theme of the company both as a companion and as an enterprise of the people of Alberta.

Typically the exchange contained three major areas of activity, namely: a public reception area where access to a public phone was provided and where business was transacted, the administration and switchboard area, and the equipment room where the system's maintenance took place. Unlike many of the exchanges, there were no living quarters provided. Employees in this exchange served St. Paul and the rural area around it as part of the province-wide long distance network linking Edmonton to rural Alberta.

The replica constructed at Fort Edmonton Park includes a generic industrial-style building at the rear which houses a collection of AGT artifacts and provides a programme activity site. Its stucco exterior is typical of a popular building trend in the 1920s.

THE AL RASCHID MOSQUE was built in 1938 at 108 Avenue and 102 Street, the present site of Victoria Composite High School. When the land on which it stood was required for the school in 1946, the mosque was moved a short distance away to 111 Avenue and 102 Street.

Muslim Canadians were recorded as early as the 1871 Census, but the greatest influx did not start until the turn of the century. Muslims from Lebanon, Turkey and Syria came to start a new life in Canada and to escape conscription into the Turkish army. Early settlers came to the West to set up homesteads but some also worked as peddlers, fur traders, or on the railways. In the 1930s the first four Muslim families in Edmonton ran rooming houses, a taxi company, a hotel and one man was a fur trader. Muslims were integrating into the British Canadian lifestyle to such a degree that some were becoming concerned about the loss of their Muslim culture. As a result, the Muslim Women's Association embarked on a fund raising campaign to build a mosque in Edmonton. Their efforts were realized in 1938 when the Al Raschid Mosque, the first in Canada, was completed. This was not only a place for worship, but a centre for religious festivals, ceremonies, box socials, and community dinners, and people of all faiths from the community were often invited to join in

The Mosque on 111 Avenue

continued on next page

THE AL RASCHID MOSQUE (continued)

The Muslim population of the city continued to grow, and in 1981 the Canadian Islamic Centre opened at 130 Avenue and 113 Street. The new centre was built on city-owned land which was given to the Muslim community in exchange for the 111 Avenue site which the city required for the proposed expansion of the Royal Alexandra Hospital. The state of the economy meant a delay in the construction of the hospital's addition, a situation which preserved the mosque from demolition. When the building finally had to be moved in 1992, it was relocated to Fort Edmonton Park.

The Al Raschid Mosque is the first mosque built in Canada. It enjoyed continuous use from its construction in 1938 until the building of the Canadian Islamic Centre in 1981.

THE MELLON FARM. The Mellon farmhouse is an example of a prairie farm house of the 1920s. The Mellon family did not live in this house themselves, but rented it to other families.

The farmhouse is the original house built in 1922 on the property of John J. Mellon on the west side of Whitemud Creek near the present Sixty-third Avenue. The 408 acres of land owned by Mr. Mellon included the present site of Fort Edmonton Park. The house was moved to 1920 Street from its original location.

The Mellon farmhouse on its original site

THE MOTORDROME. In the years immediately following the First World War, the automobile steadily began to replace horse-drawn forms of transportation. In Alberta, automobile registrations rose from 29,250 in 1921 to 65,101 in 1926. Encouraged by the development of the automobile and improvements to roads, people began moving from crowded city centres to more spacious suburban neighbourhoods.

The Motordrome

With the increase in the number of automobiles came the need for new businesses such as car dealerships, gas stations, and repair shops. The dealership-repair shops often had spacious, well-lit show rooms in the front of the building with a service or work area in the rear. Many had gas pumps and parts and accessories counters as well.

The Motordrome Ltd. was built in October, 1919 and remained in business at 10131 - 103 Street until 1926. With its peaked façade, stone inset motif, and stylized geometric stone detail, the building is a good example of the early use of geometric motifs. Later in the decade, these linear influences would be highly stylized into a new design form called *Art Deco*. When it opened, the Motordrome Ltd. offered a wide range of services including new and used automobile sales, a repair service, automobile storage, a car wash, accessory sales, and a street front gas pump. It was advertised as Edmonton's modern garage.

The replica of the Motordrome in Fort Edmonton Park serves as a restoration and display centre for antique vehicles.

STRATHCONA STREETCAR BARN, originally constructed at what is now 110 Street and 83rd Avenue, represents the south side barn of the Edmonton Radial Railway. Constructed in 1908 and opened in 1909, the facility housed streetcars operating on Edmonton's south side. Inspection of the cars and light repairs were carried out in this facility, but major repairs meant a trip to the main carbarn, Cromdale, in the north end of the city. The Strathcona Streetcar Barn was taken out of service in 1921.

In addition to the eastern section of the streetcar barn in the Park which reproduces the original carbarn, a section similar in design has been added to provide additional storage space for streetcars and work space for the members of the Edmonton Radial Railway Society, all volunteers, who collect, restore, maintain, and operate the streetcars in the Park.

Street railway service in Fort Edmonton Park began on June 10, 1984. In an average season, the society's streetcars carry well over 100,000 passengers and travel some 4000 miles. In its first ten years of operation the society's streetcars carried over a million passengers.

Strathcona streetcar barn

TRAIN STATION. The train station, while not based on a particular structure, is typical of railway depots found in small prairie cities. At Fort Edmonton Park, this building serves as a transition area through which visitors pass and are then transported back into Edmonton's history. The train station is a fitting introduction to Edmonton's past, for nowhere in Canada did the railways play a greater role in the settlement and economic development of a region than in the west.

The building conveys the stylized features of a typical depot, although the functional layout of the interior is designed to accommodate park admission booths, a gift shop, washrooms, and administrative offices. The structure is characteristic of stations built during the 1920s when the use of stucco was very popular. The bellcast hip roof includes indented hip dormers, while the extended awning is supported by heavy, thick brackets, and a hexagonal bay juts out onto the typical wooden platform. A high concrete foundation protects the lower stucco wall from baggage wagons.

In smaller stations found in towns and villages the second floor would be inhabited by the station agent's family, but in larger centres or at a divisional point, this space would house the division's administrative offices. Typically, the main floor would contain freight and baggage rooms, waiting rooms, a ticket office, and sometimes a lunchroom and kitchen.

The railway station at Fort Edmonton Park

THE FREIGHT SHED, located just north of the railway station, is a replica of the facility which the Canadian Pacific Railway built in small communities throughout the prairies. Shipments addressed to people in the area would be delivered to the freight shed by railway freight car. These shipments would then be picked up by horse and wagon, in later years by truck, and delivered to the customer's home or place of business.

The freight shed at the Park is the home of the Edmonton Model Railroad Association. Instead of cases of freight, the building contains a large HO (models built to a scale of 3.5 millimetres to each foot of the prototype) model railroad built by the club's members. Viewing areas have been installed at each end of the shed, and visitors are encouraged to come in and watch the trains.

The Edmonton Model Railroad Association, founded in 1946, built its first model railway in the old Edmonton Gardens. After eighteen years at the Gardens, the association moved to the Lions' Centre located on 112 Street where it operated its railway for the next eight years. In 1980, the association agreed to sponsor the construction of a freight shed in Fort Edmonton Park to house a new model railway display which would be open to the public. The building was turned over to Fort Edmonton Park on January 21, 1992.

The freight shed

97

BLATCHFORD FIELD HANGAR. Out of the First World War in Europe came improvements in mechanical technology such as the aeroplane. A new breed of young men returned home who would go on to become heroes of the Canadian north - the bush pilots. In 1919 Wilfrid R. (Wop) May founded Edmonton's first commercial airplane company, May Airlines Ltd., and soon the Edmonton Aviation Company came after it. The new companies carried mail, passengers, and freight, and, occasionally, barnstormed, in order to survive financially.

The original Blatchford Field Hangar

The planes took off and landed on a farmer's field in the Hagman estate, the site of the present Municipal airport. The planes were put out of business for a time in 1923 when the farm was seized by the city of Edmonton for tax arrears. In 1926 the city petitioned Ottawa to recognize the Hagman estate as an air harbour. It was subsequently licensed as the first municipally owned and operated public air harbour in Canada. The new facility, named Blatchford Field after Mayor Kenneth Blatchford, opened in 1927.

BLATCHFORD FIELD HANGAR (continued)

After a famous mercy flight in December, 1928, when Wop May and Vic Horner flew a supply of antitoxin to a small northern community in sub-zero weather, the public gave its support to the expansion of the field. Blatchford Field Hangar was built in 1929, part of a modern airport. Owing to widespread mining and oil exploration in the north, the airport became a focal point of aviation in Western Canada giving Edmonton its reputation as the *Gateway to the North*.

The reproduction of Blatchford Field Air Hangar at the Park is the Fort Edmonton Historical Foundation's newest exciting project! The Foundation, the non-profit entity incorporated to raise funds to develop Fort Edmonton Park, hopes to build the historic 1929 Blatchford Hangar to enhance the appearance of 1920 Street and to replace the temporary special events tent currently on site. Based on the original blueprints in the Provincial Archives of Alberta, the exterior of the reconstructed Blatchford Field Hangar at the Park will reproduce the features of the earlier structure, while the interior's modern facilities will include a large area to be used for special events, displays, rental facilities, and as an all-round activity space in inclement weather. Construction will begin on the Hangar once funds in excess of $2.7 million have been raised.

If you are interested in contributing to this worthwhile project, please call the Foundation's office at 496-6977.

Original Locations of some 1905 and 1920 Street buildings.

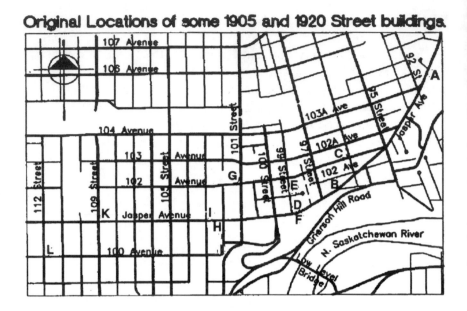

Buildings shown on the map

A. McDonald Homestead (1885 era)
B. Ernest Brown Studio (1905 era)
C. Ukrainian Book Store (1920 era)
D. Bank of Montreal (1905 era)
E. Fire Hall #1 (1905 era)
F. Post Office (1905 era)
G. Penny Arcade (1905 era)
H. Reed's Bazaar (1905 era)
I. Motordrome (1920 era)
J. Masonic Hall (1905 era)
K. Sun Drugs/ Bill's Confectionery (1920 era)
L. Ramsay's Florists (1905 era)

DONORS

The Fort Edmonton Historical Foundation acknowledges the contributions of the following companies, organizations, and individuals who through their generous donations have helped to make Fort Edmonton Park possible. While others have been generous in their contributions to Fort Edmonton Park, those persons and organizations listed below have donated at least $5000.

FORT

Palisade Walls	Alberta Energy
Rowand House	Junior League of Edmonton
	The Minerva Foundation
Watch Tower	Colonel H. Sanders Charitable Organization
Clerks' Quarters	Colonel H. Sanders Charitable Organization
Married Mens' Quarters	Sunwapta Broadcasting
Blacksmith Shop	MacCosham Van Lines
Meat Store House	Canada Packers Foundation
Ice House	The London Society
Trade Store	Hudson's Bay Company
Bake Oven	I.O.D.E Edmonton House Chapter
York Boat Shed and Mini Park	Northwestern Utilities Ltd.
Boat Shed	Edmonton Motors Ltd.
Lake and Creek	Alberta Gas Trunk Line
	Recreation Parks and Wildlife Foundation

1885 STREET

Bellerose School	Alberta Teachers' Association
James McDonald Carpentry Shop	Edmonton Construction Association
Byrnes' Shoe Shop	Colonel H. Sanders Charitable Organization

Secord Complex

McDougall General Store

Jasper House hotel

NWMP Gun Shed

Dominion Land Office

McCauley Livery Stable
Peter Erasmus House
Daly's Drug Store
Dr. Wilson's Office
McDougall Methodist Church
Kernohan's Millinery
Hutchings and Riley's
    Harness Shop
Bulletin Building

1905 STREET

St. Anthony's Catholic Church
    and School
Gyro Park
Reed's Bazaar
Ernest Brown Studio
Fire Hall #1/Civic Centre
Bank of Montreal
Law Office
Ramsay Greenhouse
Bandshell
Penny Arcade
Masonic Hall
Firkins House

Labatt's Alberta Brewery
Secord and Company Ltd.
The Secord Family
Junior League of Edmonton
McDougall and Secord Ltd.
Edmonton Automobile and
    Good Roads Association
Rotary Club of West Edmonton
Colonel H. Sanders Charitable
    Organization
Alberta Land Surveyors'
    Association
Yellow Cab Ltd.
Jack D. Edworthy and Family
Clifford E. Lee Foundation
Alberta Medical Association
McDougall United Church
Beta Sigma Phi

Edmonton South Lions Club
Canadian Imperial Bank of
    Commerce

Knights of Columbus
Southgate Developments Ltd.
Gyro Clubs of Edmonton
Reed's China and Gift Shops
Imperial Oil Ltd.
75th Anniversary Committee
Bank of Montreal
Edmonton Bar Association
Frank and Joan Tyler
Edmonton South Lions Clubs
Stuart Olson Construction
Ionic Club
Rod and Audrey Karpetz
Edmonton Community
    Foundation

Donors

Rutherford House — Canada West Insurance
Ithacan Development Corporation

St. Michael and All Angels Anglican Church — Lakeview Foundation
Henderson Homestead — Pearson Family
A. J. Toane
Rotary Club of South Edmonton

1920 STREET

Memorial Garden — George Shipley
Women's Canadian Club of Edmonton

Legion Fountain — Royal Canadian Legions
Ukrainian Bookstore — Members of the Ukrainian community

Tom Thumb Miniature Golf Course — Edmonton Northlands
Sun Drug Store/ Bill's Confectionery — Northern Alberta Dairy Pool (Dairyland)
Alberta Pharmaceutical Association
Pharmacy Historical Society
Edmonton Community Foundation
Ladies Pharmaceutical Auxiliary

AGT Telephone Exchange — Alberta Government Telephones Ltd. (AGT)

Motordrome — Rotary Club of South Edmonton

Strathcona Streetcar Barn — Edmonton Real Estate Board

OTHER

E. Y. & P. Railway — A & B Rail
CN Rail
Peter Pocklington
T. W. Graham

Locomotive Shed	Maclab Enterprises
Freight Shed	Edmonton Model Railroad Association
Train Station	Rotary Clubs of Edmonton
Street Railway	Edmonton Radial Railway Society
Landscaping	Alberta Nursery Trades Association
Belgian Horses	MacCosham Van Lines

PHOTOGRAPHIC CREDITS

The Fort Edmonton Historical Foundation would like to express its sincere appreciation to the following organizations who have been kind enough to grant permission to make use of their photographs in this guidebook. In every case, the number immediately before the colon (:) refers to the page on which the photograph is located. The number following the colon is the catalogue number of the photograph (where one is used).

British Columbia Archives and Records Service
16: A 67-505

City of Edmonton Archives
13: EA-10-1177; 21: EA-10-2955; 22: EA-10-2273; 34: EA 10-3039; 36 (upper and lower): EA-10-716; 40 (upper): EA-74-21; 41: EA-74-16; 48 (upper): EA-10-2616; 48 (lower): EA-10-1567; 54 (lower): EA 13-5; 57: EA-517-312; 60 (upper): EA 359-2; 60 (lower): EA 80-4; 61: EA-160-540; 62: EA 82-5; 66: EA 10-2287; 72: EA-211-5; 73: EA 500-19; 76: EA 500-304; 81: EA 500-19; 82: EA-1-13; 83: EA 10-220; 90: EA 118-19; 93: EA 82-1; 94: EA 160-211; 98: **XXX**

Cowan, Douglas
27

Edmonton Parks and Recreation - Fort Edmonton Park
19; 25; 31; 38; 42; 53; 71

Edmonton Journal
63: August 8, 1992, page E2

Fort Edmonton Historical Foundation
Front cover; rear cover; 64; 73; 84; 86; 91

Glenbow Museum and Archives
67: McDermid Collection, NC-6-902; 87: McDermid Collection, NC-6-10122, detail; 95: McDermid Collection, AS 73-3

Keith, William
96

National Archives of Canada
9:Charles Horetzky, PA-009240; 17:W. Kippen, Maj., PA-007476

Parker, Douglas
40; 80; 97

Provincial Archives of Alberta
20: A-2336 detail; 39: A1821; 88: BL59; 92: G1926

Brown Collection
10: B6608; 28:B1043; 29:B4756; 32: B8347; 33: B4593; 35 (upper): B7126; 35 (lower): B4110; 37 (upper): B8400; 37 (lower): B783; 43 (upper): B4156; 43 (lower): B8257; 44: B8428; 45: B4756 detail; 46: B4756 detail; 47 (upper): B5703; 47 (lower): B8488; 49: B9989; 50: B5560; 51:B9983; 52: B5714; 57: B5030; 65: B4964; 68: B1342; 69: B4122; 70: B5050; 75: B4598; 77: B1934; 79: B6210

Saskatchewan Archives Board
24: R-A4050

FOR FURTHER READING

Regrettably, some of the books listed below are now out of print.

Babcock, D. *A Gentleman of Strathcona.* Calgary: University of Calgary Press,1989.

Cashman, Tony. *The Best Edmonton Stories.* Edmonton: Hurtig, 1976.

Fort Edmonton Historical Foundation. *Edmonton: the Way It Was.* Edmonton: The Foundation, 1977.

Gilpin, John. *Edmonton, Gateway to the North.* Woodland Hills, CA: Windsor Press, 1984.

Gordey, Catherine. *Women Pioneers of Alberta.* Edmonton: University of Alberta, 1974.

Hatcher, Colin and Tom Schwarzkopf. *Edmonton's Electric Transit.* Toronto: Railfare Enterprises, 1983.

Kane, Paul. *Wanderings of an artist among the Indians of North America, from Canada to Vancouver's Island and Oregon, through the Hudson's Bay company's territory and back again.* Orig, publ. 1859. Reprint Edmonton: M. G. Hurtig, 1968.

MacDonald, Jac. *Historic Edmonton: an architectural and historical guide.* Edmonton: Lone Pine, 1987.

MacDonald, Janice E. *The Northwest Fort: Fort Edmonton.* Edmonton: Lone Pine, 1983.

MacGregor, James G. *Edmonton: A History.* Edmonton: Hurtig, 1967.

- - *Edmonton Trader, the story of John A. McDougall.* Toronto: McClelland and Stewart, 1963.

For further reading

- - *The Klondike Rush Through Edmonton. 1897-1898.* Toronto: McClelland and Stewart, 1970.

McDonald, George H. *Edmonton: Fort - House - Factory.* Edmonton: Douglas Printing, 1959.

Newman, Peter. *Caesars of the Wilderness*, vol. ii of *Company of Adventurers.* New York: Viking, 1987.

- - *Company of Adventurers,* vol. i. New York: Viking, 1985.

Person, Dennis and Carin Routledge. *Edmonton. Portrait of a City.* Edmonton: Reidmore, 1981.

Rawlinson, H. E. "Chief Factor - John Rowand." *Alberta Historical Review,* 1975.

Rogers, Edith. *History Made in Edmonton.* Edmonton: E. Rogers, 1975.

INDEX

Notes

Notes

1920 Street

Notes

114

Notes

1920 Street

Notes

Notes

1920 Street

Notes

The Fort Edmonton Historical Foundation

The Fort Edmonton Historical Foundation, incorporated December 18, 1969, grew out of the vision and efforts of a group of early pioneers who wished to preserve the history of Edmonton in a living history museum. The museum was to be dedicated to Edmontonians, past, present, and future. Their dream has been realized in the development of Fort Edmonton Park.

With initial funding provided by the Rotary Clubs of Edmonton and a master plan provided by the City of Edmonton, Fort Edmonton Park began to grow. Twenty-five years later, with the financial and volunteer support of many committed businesses, citizens, and governments, the Fort Edmonton Historical Foundation has contributed over six million dollars to the capital development of Fort Edmonton Park.

To achieve its mission of ensuring that Fort Edmonton Park continues to grow as a living history museum, the Foundation works in partnership with donors, sponsors, and the City of Edmonton to provide the financial and human resources that will help Fort Edmonton Park grow and continue to be a quality living history museum.

Now, with a revised master plan, the Foundation is continuing to raise money for the completion of Fort Edmonton Park. Looking to the future for the Park, the Foundation will complete 1920 Street which will depict Edmonton as a developing city, and which will celebrate Edmonton's achievements and leadership in commerce, government, agriculture, communication, and aviation.

You can become a part of the continued development and preservation of Edmonton's history by participating in one of the many special events of the Foundation. Community support is vital to the Foundation's continuing success. Donations may be sent to Box 5369, Stn. WECC, Edmonton, AB, T5P 4C9. If you wish more information on the Fort Edmonton Historical Foundation and its activities, or if you would like to receive our newsletter, please call the Foundation's office at (403) 496-6977.

**Fort Edmonton Historical
Foundation**

**An Illustrated Guide to
Fort Edmonton Park**

Additional copies are available
from the Foundation:

Box 5369,
Postal Station W.E.C.C.
Edmonton, Alberta, Canada
T5P 4C9

ISBN 0-920805-03-5

published by:

**Havelock House
Victoria, British Columbia**